## Palace of Varieties

Julian Critchley, Conservative MP for Alder-shot, was first elected to Parliament in 1959. His most recent books are the bestselling *Westminster Blues* and *Heseltine: The Unauthorised Biography*. He is married and lives in Farnham, Surrey.

# PALACE OF VARIETIES

*An insider's view of Westminster*

## JULIAN CRITCHLEY

*faber and faber*

First published in 1989
by John Murray (Publishers) Ltd,
This revised paperback edition first published in 1990
by Faber and Faber Limited
3 Queen Square London WC1N 3AU

Printed in Great Britain by Cox & Wyman Ltd,
Reading, Berkshire

A CIP record for this book is available from the British Library

ISBN 0–571–16138–3

# Contents

# 1
# *Better than Working*

WHAT SORT of people become Members of Parliament? Who has not glimpsed on television in the aftermath of an election, an interview with the eager victor, flanked by his wife and party agent, poised before the gates of New Palace Yard? The brand-new MP pledges loyalty not only to his companions (both of whom will stand in need of it) but also to his party which has provided his ticket to ride. He may even mumble something about loyalty to his country. The camera cuts away leaving the rest of his great day to our imagination.

I was in that happy position in October 1959. I had been elected for Rochester and Chatham in Kent, defeating, much to my delight and surprise, the sitting Labour MP, Arthur Bottomley. 'Arthur' had won the seat in 1945 and had hung on against the odds in three general elections. In 1959 he had lost by a thousand votes. I had been wafted into Westminster at the age of 28 on Harold Macmillan's coat-tails. I was an undeserving example of what was then the start of a new wave of Conservatives. I was first-generation public school, Shrewsbury, and Pembroke College, Oxford. I had no money, working as I did for several advertising agencies as a trainee account executive. My salary was in the range of £900 a year. I was married with a two-year-old daughter and lived in a tiny flat rented from Morden College in Blackheath. I drove a Ford Prefect which had been lent to me by a friendly Chatham garage owner. I was quite unknown outside – that is, outside the narrow confines of those young Tories whose hobby was politics and whose ambition was to win a seat in the House of Commons. Thanks to the voters, I had fallen on my feet.

1

The explanation for such good fortune lay in my adoption in 1957 by the Rochester and Chatham Tories as their prospective parliamentary candidate. I had little to offer save energy, a quality which the handful of party activists who made up the selection committee knew, through bitter experience, to be the most important requirement of all. My chances, they must have known, were slim, and the choice of candidates from whom they might choose a standard-bearer, limited. Men in middle life with political ambition were looking for more winnable seats; local Tory parties in places such as Chatham were offered a selection of 'professional' candidates-to-be, young men like me who had risen through the ranks of the Young Conservatives.

To become the prospective parliamentary candidate for any seat, safe, marginal or hopeless, it was essential to have one's name upon the Central Office list of prospective candidates. This I had achieved in 1956 when Sir Donald Kaberry MP, the then Vice-Chairman of the party in charge of candidates, granted me a cheerful interview. He would insist that he knew my father, 'Brigadier Critchley of the Greyhounds'. I tried to put him right, but without success. Whatever the misunderstandings, I was added to the list on the strength not of achievement, for I had done nothing, but on my record as an active Young Conservative in Paris, Hampstead and London, and my exploits among the Tories of Oxford. It was good of Donald to have added my name to his list. I suspect he did so in the knowledge that we were unlikely ever to see each other again.

The new wave of candidates, to which I have referred, soon became a flood. In 1959, the Tory party backbencher was quite different from what he has become today. The Labour Party, too, has changed. As politics has become sharper under Mrs Thatcher, and the consensus has disappeared, so, ironically perhaps, the parties have converged socially. Politics has become a middle-class activity. As Mrs Thatcher has gone up in the world so the Conservative party has come down in it.

In the late 'fifties, the Tory party was well suited. Lawyers in black jackets and striped pants jostled for place on the Government benches with company directors whose uniform consisted of blue serge, cream silk shirts (some had daringly abandoned the detached stiff white collar) and discreet neckties. Shoes were

2

invariably a well-shone black and handkerchiefs, white. The Knights of the Shires sat next to the members of the professional classes united by a bond of shared experience at school, in the services and at the London clubs. Many, if not most of them, had gone into politics as an extension of their sense of social obligation with no thought of ministerial office or of preferment.

Into this company of bumble bees was inserted a small number of wasps. The general election of 1950 had seen the election of a group of the most able recruits: Enoch Powell, Iain Macleod, Edward Heath and Reginald Maudling, high achievers of the middle class, an essential reinforcement to the ranks of Government. When Churchill came to power in May 1940 he had imposed his will upon the Tory party. He promoted his friends. 'Chamberlainites' who had bitterly opposed him, and had conspired to unseat him in his constituency immediately before the outbreak of war (Churchill, incidentally, was 're-selected' by one vote), were relegated, in the main, to the backbenches where their patriotism could flourish in secret session. Churchill was followed as Premier by Anthony Eden, and Eden by Macmillan. With the exception of 'Rab' Butler, who changed sides, it might be asserted that the Tory front bench in the years after the end of the war consisted of Churchill and his supporters; the backbenches were the home of the Chamberlainites. The class of 1950 served to reinforce the front at the expense of the backbenches. The Chamberlainites were to re-emerge in 1975 under the guise of 'Thatcherites', taking power in the leadership election of that year in what has become known as 'the Peasants' Revolt'.

The paths to Parliament have never been clearly signposted. The young victor of some provincial by-election seems to the public at large to have popped up from nowhere, a name, hitherto unknown, which has, by some mysterious process, found itself upon a ballot paper. The truth is that in mainland Britain politics is a minority activity. Psephologists claim that only 2 per cent of the population bother to join a political party and an even smaller proportion devote their time and energies to politicking. It is a wonder that the Labour and Conservative parties do not pick candidates whose views are even more extreme than they presently are. The British political system works by electing the unknown to Parliament at the behest of

3

the unrepresentative. We are lucky it works as well as it does.

The newly elected MP, emerging from this arcane process into the lights of the cameras, appears for a moment as if he were under close arrest. On one hand stands his party agent who can certainly claim some credit for what the newspapers will be calling 'a famous victory'. On the other will be his long-suffering wife. The party agent stands as symbol of the party system, for it is today impossible to be elected to Parliament without the say-so of a political party. The last Independent MP was elected as long ago as 1945. His wife stands as symbol of sacrifices made and threatened, for the divorce rate among MPs is high.

The party agent will, if he is employed by the Conservative party, know his place. Agents, with the exception of Anthony Durrant, the MP for Reading West, do not pass the green baize door which separates the Member from the party organisation. (Durrant's first job was as a commis-waiter at the Connaught Hotel.) This distinction is not to be found in the Labour and Liberal parties. In the Conservative party, the constituency agent is an organiser not an activist. Labour agents, on the other hand, are often the political driving force locally. Tories raise money through social functions: socialists and Liberals engage in political activity as if they, too, were one of the lads.

I have long enjoyed a love/hate relationship with the Conservative party. I was not converted or even convinced. I quite simply could have joined none other. My family was medical, and there were then no Tories like most doctors. My grandparents were poor but proud. My paternal grandfather, a clerk in the Bristol Gas Works, was a passionate Tory who hated Ernie Bevin. My maternal grandfather was a railwayman whose religion – he was an Anglican – ensured his allegiance to the 'squires' party' in turn-of-the-century Shropshire. I was given a conventional fee-paying education at schools where to be a Conservative was the norm. At Oxford I joined forces with the young Michael Heseltine whose origins were similar. To have become a Liberal would have been to opt out of parliamentary politics; to have joined Labour would have been unthinkable. The Conservative party in the shape of its chairman, Lord Woolton, had recently let down ladders of opportunity into the tennis-playing suburbs up which, as children of the new middle class, we eagerly scrambled. It can also be said that the Tory party itself, ever on the look-out for the young and promising, was only too happy to take us at our own estimation.

The Conservative party can boast of being the most successful democratic political party in the world. It is certainly the longest lived. It used to be the party of the upper class which, while taking care to recruit into its ranks the brighter members of the middle, relied for its electoral success upon the votes of the deferential working class. Until recently it was not an ideological party, although in the past it had torn itself apart in disputes over free trade versus protection, and over rearmament before Hitler's War. It has a tradition of relative tolerance. Dissent even now is not punished by expulsion or even by a conspiracy to bring about de-selection within the constituency; dissent is regarded as a luxury which is paid for in the coin of neglect. In a party in which the great majority of its MPs are thirsting for office, failure to win promotion can be punishment enough.

Thus the Tory party remains, as is Labour, a broad coalition, the 'broad church' to which political commentators so often refer. Its span can stretch as far as Critchley on the left and Terry Dicks on the right, with the bulk of the party taking its cue from the prevailing orthodoxy of conviction politics and Thatcherite 'radicalism'. Tories who are obviously 'left' are in a minority, their numbers balanced by a small group of committed right-wingers. In the early 'eighties, the Labour party lost its social democrats (or the bulk of them) to a new party led by the Gang of Four. The Conservative party, despite being subjected to similar internal strains, stayed ostensibly united, losing only one of its MPs to the Social Democrats. The 'wets' withdrew into their tents from the mouths of which they would occasionally give tongue to what many of them would describe as the 'longest political hijack in history'.

A career in politics demands no qualifications of any kind. No examination is necessary. Demand for places at Westminster always exceeds the supply, although the party has little influence over the quality of applicants. The politically ambitious thrust themselves forward regardless of merit. It could reasonably be asserted that the more intelligent among the political classes sit the civil service examination or gravitate eventually to teaching political science at university or even to writing about politics for the national press. The parties have a vivid interest in attracting talent to themselves, the more so as it is the custom to fill the ranks of the executive from the elected members of the legislature. Yet there is no way the more able can be persuaded to abandon whatever it is they happen to be doing in favour of an uncertain career in politics in which the hours are unsocial and the chances of success uncertain. Those who deplore the quality of MPs or even the standard of debate, which is much lower than in the Lords, can only ponder the consequences of a system in which the bulk of the people care little about politics, and its practioners pick themselves.

What then are the qualities necessary to be a Member of Parliament? Moral rectitude is clearly important. MPs are rarely if ever corrupted, a state of affairs which the cynical might attribute to the powerlessness of the run-of-the-mill backbench MP. If there is corruption to be found in public life, it is more likely to lurk in local government. MPs cannot grant planning permission. Nevertheless, the cynic would be wrong in his assessment. Most MPs are incorruptible, at least in a financial sense, although a few may fiddle their motoring expenses. Unlike American television evangelists whose stock in trade is hellfire interspersed with appeals for money from the gullible, Members of Parliament lack both the glamour and the opportunity. If we are vulnerable it is to the small cheques of the BBC which we receive in return for a fleeting appearance on 'Today'.

The principal quality necessary for success in politics is a religious temperament – that is faith without scrutiny. The party whips, recruited as they are from amongst backbench MPs, do like to know where they are. The 'candidate-minister', to borrow and adapt a Soviet phrase, has to satisfy the whips, and the Chief Whip in particular, that he has ability and that he is 'sound'. Able people are usually clever; clever chaps are not necessarily able in the sense that they are capable of the sustained application that is necessary to get things done. And the 'clever' are unlikely to have the religious temperament. Ability/cleverness can be demonstrated either on the floor of the House or upstairs in committee.

Sound MPs are those who put their party first. Or, to put it in another way, those whose reactions to an event can be confidently predicted. The true believer is more likely to be found in political parties that contain a high ideological content. 'Thatcherites' are easily called to arms. The Labour party's Campaign Group carries with it a touchstone of belief against which events may be tested. In the same way when Britain's entry into Europe was top of the agenda, the Europeans, who were drawn from all parties, were as passionate in their beliefs as the antis. Ideology is not the only party cement. Loyalty has long been believed to be the Tory party's secret weapon, and there is no doubt that it was party loyalty which bound Harold Macmillan's party together, until, that is, the Profumo affair. In the same way Edward Heath's position as party leader went unchallenged until defeats at two elections dissolved the cement.

The ambitious politician-to-be must possess other qualities, too. The candidate must above all be persistent. He must sleep with his suitcase packed, ready at the ring of the telephone to quit hearth and home for a meeting of a constituency selection committee in shire and suburb. Sir Geoffrey Howe and Sir Leon Brittan must between them have visited as many small towns up and down the length of Britain as did J. B. Priestley in the years before the war. Others win prizes in the political lottery at their first draw. I cannot say what it is specifically that Labour party selection conferences seek from those who parade before them, but I have a clear idea what it is that Tories do.

Conservatives want two for the price of one. Wives are important, much more so than in the People's Party. A friend of mine fought three general elections as a Labour candidate with three different wives: no one noticed. I was selected for Aldershot in 1969 partly because my wife ('a damned fine woman' in the eyes of a Hampshire Colonel) stood up to answer the question asked of all three wives. She was educated at Cheltenham. The Tory party makes much of the Union Jack and of the family, and its members feel it important that their standard should be borne into battle by an ostensibly loving couple. Bachelors, gay or not, generally receive shorter shrift.

So far I have listed, as qualities needed for political success, honesty, predictability and persistence. Matrimony can only be described as a happy accident. But more is necessary. The successful politician must have the skin of a rhinoceros and the

7

stamina of a horse. The sensitive will suffer acutely from the abuse of his enemies (in politics you are either flattered or abused), the jibes of his colleagues and the crassness of at least one of his local newspapers. His motives will be misunderstood and his comments misinterpreted. Sooner, or later, he will come a cropper in the House, and the Commons chamber can be merciless. He will unconsciously or not offend the chairman of his constituency party, his agent and the editor of the *Aldershot Bugle*. If he decides on a point of principle to stand firm on an issue, the restoration of capital punishment, for example, he may have to dig deep into his reserves. Moral fibre was something about which my preparatory school headmasters used to make much. It can come in handy.

Stamina is essential. High horsepower is needed to cope with the long hours, the tedium and, if one becomes a junior minister, the grindingly hard work. Ability is not considered to be enough. His colleagues were always accusing Reginald Maudling of being lazy, a charge which Maudling's friends would angrily refute. Reggie may have had a Rolls-Royce mind but his rivals could not forgive his laid-back approach. The work-load of a middle-ranking minister is very heavy indeed. He will be at the Ministry from 9 till 6. He will be at the Commons from 6 to 11: at weekends he will be nursing his constituency. Backbenchers can, to some extent, pick and choose. We may be asked to hang around the building in case the division bells ring, but we can fill the long hours in any way we like. And the long months of vacation are totally ours. Ministers snatch three weeks in the summer before returning to Whitehall to mind the shop.

MPs are not well paid. In 1990 the salary was raised to £26,701 in line with a grade of the civil service. This is the equivalent of the £400 a year first paid to MPs in 1910. The same amount of money is available as Secretarial and Research Allowance, and there is no rule against employing relatives. Many MPs do employ their wives, but no doubt at some cost. There are demands that can be made on secretaries that cannot be made on wives, and vice versa, and breakfast-time silences are not conducive to the swift dispatch of constituency business. Most MPs double their salary by taking outside work, proper moonlighting whereby journalists write, lawyers practise law and company directors manage. Backbenchers blessed with the gift of the gab can become celebrities, famous for being simply themselves. Such celebrities can make pocket money working a summer season of radio quiz shows ('Out of Order'), appearing on 'Newsnight' (poorly and slowly paid) and making trips to draughty West Country village halls to take part in 'Any Questions' at £150 a time. Some of us have even appeared on 'Desert Island Discs' which is the ultimate accolade of public life.

What then makes men and women go into politics? The answer must be a combination of service and ambition. Ambition is, as Henry Fairlie has written, 'the engine of the public good' and there is no necessity to apologise for it. Service is the desire to do something to improve the lot of fellow citizens, or indeed of the country. When it comes to individuals it would be unwise to attempt to measure the quantities of the equation. It is enough to assert that service and ambition are the twin reasons for embarking on public life. Politics is an acquired taste, shared, as we have already noted, by only a small minority. The majority seem content to leave the game to others, willing to vote at infrequent elections and happy to call down a plague on all three houses. Nothing bores the public more than the partisan. The presence of two opposing backbenchers on a village brainstrust who can be relied upon to slag each other off, a vulgar phrase which expresses a widely held contempt, often induces gloom. Yet the political parties are essential to the workings of a parliamentary democracy. We cannot avoid a three-week election campaign held every four and a half years: what we can escape is force-feeding.

Politics is a glamorous activity. Leading politicians enjoy much social prestige. Mrs Thatcher may be loved or loathed but she is never overlooked. As Prime Minister she wields power. Not for her Macmillan's self-deprecatory remark about power being 'a Dead Sea fruit'. She lives a life of frantic activity, existing at a pace which would exhaust most people. She boasts of her ability to get by with only four hours' sleep and is pleased to be described as a workaholic. Her habits must cause her intimates much pain – bed by 2.30 a.m. – but as Prime Minister she must be indulged. In compensation for doing what comes naturally Mrs Thatcher is freed of money worries, transported swiftly to the ends of the earth, fed, served and watered. Her style may not be that of other politicians but she remains a good advertisement for the calling. That a grocer's daughter from Grantham and a 'second-class chemist' can rise to world fame, and in the process get the better of most men, is, I suppose, a matter of simple national satisfaction.

What then is the prospect before the triumphant trio standing in New Palace Yard, chatting to a friendly policeman? If he owes his victory to a general election he will be one of many newcomers, all with their way to make. A by-election victor will already have been propelled into the public eye, but he is likely to be as quickly forgotten. There are 650 MPs, the majority of whom are not beyond ambition. Competition will be fierce, not so much across the House but within one's own party, where enemies lurk. The temptations to overplay a hand are great. It is not long before reputations of a sort are established. The view that so-and-so is an 'ass' can be quickly won and seldom lost. The media stands ready to give prominence to the slightest of opinions, sub-editors of great newspapers keeping lists of MPs of all parties who are known to be good for the instant quote. 'Disgusting' says a Tory MP of an issue about which he knows nothing and has thought little. Question Time offers up a thousand chances of making a fool of oneself. The all too helpful question to a beleaguered Minister, a blatant attempt to muscle in on some tragedy or a stab in the back can fix a reputation as firmly as a pin can a butterfly to a piece of card. The Commons is a minefield through which the newly elected MP must walk with a cat-like tread. The picture of wife, agent and Member at the gates of Westminster can easily capture the apogee of a political career.

The party agent must return home to take up a job which can be as thankless as it is unrewarding. The Member's wife must accustom herself to the solitary life in which she bids farewell on a Monday morning to a husband whom she will see again, exhausted, late on a Friday night. She has little to look forward to save the draw of the raffle at some fête. The victor himself has the spoils. The magic initials 'MP' are his. Was it not Trollope who wrote that it was no small honour to have the letters MP after one's name? He was right.

# 2

# Drawing the
# Raffle

THE PARTY agent who has delivered victory in the constituency becomes the third most important person in an MP's life. First is the chairman of his local party; second, his area whip, the fellow MP who as a member of the Whips' Office is responsible for the victor's conduct and voting record; and third the party agent, the paid servant of the local party whose loyalty, strictly speaking, is to the local Conservative association. The Member's wife wins no medals; she comes with the package.

Members of Parliament are known by their constituencies. I have been first 'Rochester and Chatham' and then 'Aldershot'. Just as I can spot with the eye of an eagle the word 'Critchley' in a mass of newsprint, so, too, the word 'Aldershot' will leap at me from out of the page. The identification becomes total. The sense of ownership, of territoriality, is strong: 'all this', I remember once thinking as I travelled by train through Rochester and Chatham, 'is mine'. The feeling is not reciprocated. I doubt if half the population of Rochester could have put a name to their MP in 1964, although a slightly higher proportion might have named him correctly after twenty years in Aldershot. The truth is that the MP does not matter much locally.

He has no power. The local authority can level rates, tear down buildings, grant planning permission and make the environment more or less habitable. The local paper carries weekly photographs of the Mayor, planting some tree. National politics is left to an indomitable squad of letter writers, many of whom are mad, whose tedious letters fill the correspondence columns. News of the MP surfaces from time to time. The paper may carry the gist of a hand-out from the local office of the party: 'MP defends

11

Government's record'. It may show a photograph of the MP's wife opening the annual Conservative 'Fayre'; it will certainly print the hand-outs of his rivals, the prospective Labour and Liberal candidates who will, in their turn, have been bombarding the paper with missives purporting to show knowledge and concern. The MP's speech in the House, or a part of it, will surface in the middle pages, a fortnight or so later. For most of the time constituents neither know nor care who their Member is or what he is up to. And there is no good reason why they should. Politics is very much a minority activity, and it is much to the credit of the majority that they should be impervious to the drip of assertion and supplication which is the stock in trade of so much of politics. They have much more important things to do: they simply get on with their lives.

The relationship between the MP and his local party is very different indeed. He is their Member, their choice. They have, after all, spent months choosing him, an activity which party activists hugely enjoy, and which comes, at infrequent intervals, as a reward for long nights spent 'on the knocker', canvassing the wet streets in a thankless search for votes. He has been the standard-bearer at a general election; an election which has been crowned by victory. Thanks to the energy of the few, the devoted band of front-line campaigners who actually care what happens to their country and are prepared to do something about it, the candidate has been changed into the Member of Parliament, living proof, as it were, of the rightness of their opinions and the efficacy of their electioneering. He may have been elected THE Member of Parliament for Aldershot (not the Conservative Member of Parliament, you should note, for the constitution does not recognise the existence of political parties), but such niceties cut little ice with the association.

Why does anyone join a political party? And by so doing surrender the secrecy of the ballot paper? Politics at the local level is an activity undertaken with the like-minded and with a purpose in mind. Socialists wish to change society; to right wrongs. Conservatives tend to rally to the defence of things; the existing order or their own position *vis à vis* their neighbour. Mrs Thatcher may boast of her radicalism but she leads a conservative party. Conservatives disapprove of what many of them will call

12

'politics'. Tories join their local party in order to return a Conservative government and the way to achieve that is by sending a Tory MP to Westminster.

The Conservative distaste for 'politics' as such was brought home to me in 1988 when I accepted an invitation from the Deputy Speaker, Sir Paul Dean, to speak at a dinner held in Clevedon in what was once, before the Peter Walker boundary changes, Somerset. The dinner was attended by a hundred or so of the retired members of the Avon middle class. The food was, as usual, dreadful, but the audience was good-natured enough. I spoke in favour of the televising of the House of Commons as the debate was due to take place within a fortnight. I think I failed to carry a single person with me. The questioners all feared that the cameras would encourage more, not less 'politics', the politics, that is, of our opponents. They were also certain that the cameras would complicate the Government's task, particularly in regard to the impression Mrs Thatcher might make at the twice-weekly Prime Minister's Questions.

Be that as it may. Tory associations are mainly social anyway. Funds are the means to a political end, and in order to raise money Tories lunch and dine (with a visiting speaker, it is true, asked to attend in order to deliver a sermon, which Nigel Nicolson, the son of Harold, in his perceptive book *People and Parliament* calls 'the stiffener of established faith'), hold bazaars, sell second-hand clothes and organise a grand Summer Fayre held in the most salubrious garden they can find. Life proceeds at a stately pace from one 'draw' to the next, the prizes allocated by raffle, a ceremony which has taken on an almost religious significance. Indeed, it is said that there is even a raffle at Chequers every Boxing Day on the occasion of Mrs Thatcher's famous lunch, to which are invited the most faithful of her entourage.

Most active Conservatives are women of a certain age. They are, at root, unpolitical, although they have no objection to political truisms emphatically delivered by any speaker who cares to do so. They raise the money and man the committee rooms. They discriminate against women when it comes to the selection of parliamentary candidates. They constitute the MP's praetorian guard for, with an attractive loyalty, they do tend to spring to the defence of the devil they know. They are still inclined to defer, although exceptions must be made for a scattering of their more formidable sisters, tweedy, lisle-stockinged lady magistrates into whom authority has been bred. Which brings me to the well-known picture of terrible Tory ladies.

Tory ladies gathered together in conference halls at seaside resorts out of season are the favourite butts of cartoonists of every political persuasion. They make up the bulk of the audience, awful with hats, ready to accord to the most tongue-tied Minister of the Crown his customary standing ovation: they come to life when the Conference debates capital and corporal punishment, cheering to the echo those speakers who, like the young Edwina Currie, flourish handcuffs from the rostrum. When Mrs Thatcher, clad in electric blue, makes her end-of-Conference oration, they give her a rapturous reception. Some have even be glimpsed on their feet, waving those sinister blue banners which have recently been on display at party occasions.

That is probably the worst that can be said of them. In truth they are generous to the undeserving, loyal to their leaders (a trait from which I have hugely benefited in stormy times in Aldershot) and unstridently patriotic. If their views on punishment owe more to the Old than the New Testament, it can be easily explained. Women are more vulnerable to violence, and many, who read daily of ever-rising rates of violent crime, tend to think that the answer lies in the severity of punishment. If they are beastly to prominent Tories, it is the Home Secretary of the day who becomes their sole target. I will not have a word said against Tory women: I number many among my best friends.

In the Tory party the constituency chairmanship changes every three years. The chairman or chairwoman – among Conservatives there is no nonsense about the use of the word 'chair', surely the ugliest abbreviation in the language – is one of the most important persons in an MP's political life. He is dependent upon his goodwill. Were the MP and the chairman to quarrel, or should the lines of communication between them break, a gap would open up between the Member in Parliament and the Tories in the constituency upon whom he depends not simply for support but for his eventual re-adoption as the candidate. An MP who cannot count on the friendship and thus the support of his officers has lost his 'parson's freehold', that security of tenure in safe seats which is the guarantee of his continuing political career.

The local association provides a platform for the MP which he can use to put his message over to the voters. It is one of several such platforms; over a year there will be invitations to speak to the Chamber of Commerce or to the Rotary, to the Elders' Club or the Mothers' Union, but the association remains the most important link between Westminster and the voter at large. That, at least, is the conventional wisdom. In fact, it can be less a link than a barrier, for the number of its functions (if the various ward organisations are taken into account) can be so great as to act as a filter between the MP and the public. I have spent most of my time talking to the same handful of people whose support for the party, if not their enthusiasm for me, I can usually take for granted.

The Aldershot association has fifteen hundred or so members, and little money. It is poorer than its neighbours and much smaller. Nevertheless, its members are engaged in what Nicolson calls 'the continuous process of creating mutual confidence, evolving leaders and impressing outsiders by the assumption of success.' Its officers are permitted their statutory three years in office for competition is usually far from fierce, and the candidates at the Annual General Meeting, rarely opposed. In the Tory party the local association is free to go its own way for Central Office can influence it but not dictate to it. A bargain has been implicitly struck between the party in Smith Square and the 650 local party associations: in return for the right to choose their own parliamentary candidates, local politicians leave policy-making to their 'betters' in London.

The party agent is the sole professional among a band of amateurs. He is trained by the national party, but his salary is the responsibility of the local association. A full-time agent is becoming a luxury. I have not had a professionally qualified agent for years, so poor are the Aldershot Tories. In his stead we employ a kind of super-secretary who, if one is lucky, and we are, does the job of an agent at half the money. The agent has the task of energising the locals to the extent that his salary is met and the Central Office quota regularly paid. Moneys left over will meet the running expenses of the party locally and top up the Fighting

Fund, a sum of money which rests comfortably in the building society and is used to pay for the general election. While the agent's loyalty is to his paymasters, he cannot but fail to work closely with the MP, a relationship in which mutual confidence and even affection is necessary. A good agent will act as an early warning system for the Member, tipping him off when trouble is brewing, and keeping him informed of what people are saying about him. He can judge how popular are the party's policies. Most Tory party associations spend much of their time engaged in fraternal quarrels, not over policy but over personalities. It is the agent's duty to pour oil: by the same token it is vitally important that the MP keeps out of the dog-fight and avoids taking sides.

In Rochester and Chatham I was a young man promoted above his station. Adopted as the prospective candidate at the age of 26 for what was still called a 'marginal seat', I was as green as an unripe banana. Rochester was in those days a decaying city on the Medway, graced by a Norman cathedral, and the keep of a ruined castle. The Georgian houses around the Close were lived in by the richer families of the locally based professional and commercial classes. But what gentility there was was spread thinly. Chatham still played host to the Royal Navy and the dockyard was the largest single employer. The fact that it had kept wage rates relatively low for the 8,000 or so people who worked in it was one of the reasons why the seat had stayed with Arthur Bottomley and the Labour party for so long.

Chatham was a garrison town, built in the middle years of the last century. It was a town of terraced houses which led interminably up steep hills, houses in which lived what was to all intents and purposes a pre-war working class, largely untouched by affluence. At the end of arterial roads lay the newly built housing estates, most of which were owned by the council. The Tory association was small in number and poor of purse. The city of Rochester was dominated by the Conservatives: Chatham by Labour. Rochester, however, could boast of two famous local politicians, Aldermen Skipper and Tickner. Alderman Skipper ignored the local party. He was a newsagent, wide of girth, who had served several terms as the city's mayor. Alderman Tickner was a butcher. Rivals within the council for many years, they had come to hate one another with a passion that other Conservatives kept for the common enemy. In 1957 or thereabouts there occurred the 'Battle of Abbeville'. The two Aldermen were included in a good-will visit to Rochester's twin town where, over a dinner of a standard to which they must have been unaccustomed, they came to blows. The fisticuffs were widely reported in the popular press, and the subject of much editorialising in the *Chatham News*. The 'Battle of Abbeville' thus passed into local legend, and the two contestants returned to the city's Guildhall little the worse for their contretemps.

I paid my first visit to Aldershot in 1969 after I had received a letter from the local Tories asking me if I wished to submit my name as a possible successor to Sir Eric Errington. As I had never served in the army the town was unknown territory. One glance at its rows of terraced houses built in the style common to all nineteenth-century garrison towns, and I knew I was to all intents and purposes still in Chatham. Instead of the Royal Navy, the road signs into the town all proclaimed 'Aldershot – Home of the British Army'. Should I drive sitting to attention?

While Rochester and Chatham was, in those days, a marginal seat, won by whichever party happened to win the general election, Aldershot had never been anything but a Tory seat. It had been represented in Parliament by Lord Woolmer, Oliver Lyttelton (Lord Chandos) and Sir Eric Errington, in turn. It was basically a working-class town, inhabited in large part by one-time non-commissioned officers who had set themselves up in small businesses. There was no dockyard to sustain the Labour vote. And the shopkeepers of Aldershot were Tories to a man. The political flavour of the town could have been described as 'patriotic working class'.

In 1970 the boundaries of the constituency extended well beyond Aldershot to include Farnborough, a middle-class town inhabited by aviation scientists who worked at the Royal Aircraft Establishment, and middle-ranking civil servants who commuted to London. Beyond Aldershot and Farnborough, which were later to be amalgamated by Peter Walker into the Borough of Rushmoor, were the lusher pastures of Hartley Wintney, Crondall, Odiham, Yateley (in those days a village: later to become a

17

dormitory town occupied by first-time owner-occupiers) and the military town of Fleet.

Fleet had grown in order to accommodate retired officers and their families. A small settlement of little character set down in the barren lands of Hampshire, it was the most Conservative part of the constituency. The Ladies of Fleet raised most of the money for the Aldershot Tories (in those days the association could afford the services of a full-time agent), and made up the bulk of the audience at any social or political function that we held. The president of the local Tories usually came from Fleet or from Hartley Wintney, and the chairman from Aldershot. Crondall was even grander. A widow living in Farnham once asked me why I represented a seat in the east of the county. 'The west', she said, 'is so much smarter'. I asked her how she could tell. 'By the number of admirals per village' was her answer. Crondall, in the early 'seventies, had two admirals of its very own.

By 1987, the rise in population had obliged the Boundary Commissioners to re-draw the limits of the constituency. 'Aldershot' shrank to include only 'Rushmoor', Yateley and Hartley Wintney, a contraction which did not make the seat any less Conservative but which did make the Conservative association much poorer. The Ladies of Fleet transferred their allegiance to Colonel Michael Mates, and with it their funds. The Aldershot Division became more or less an outer London suburban constituency, the bulk of its vote coming from the twin towns of Aldershot and Farnborough. If 'old' money was still to be found in Hartley Wintney, and in the adjacent villages of Rotherwick, Eversley and Mattingley, Aldershot and Farnborough had 'no' money. The 'new' money which has been attracted to the Hampshire/Surrey/Berkshire region is to be found to excess in nearby Farnham and Camberley. Indeed, 'Camberley Man' can be recognised by his jacuzzi, his time-share in Marbella and his personalised number plate.

If Aldershot is the 'Sparta' of Hampshire, then Farnham is the 'Athens' of Surrey. The army still plays an important part in the life of Aldershot. Ten thousand servicemen and their wives live within the town's boundaries. They are at their most obvious at civic functions or when a regiment or corps marches through the town to celebrate its freedom of the borough. The Parachute

Regiment comes into its own at the time of its annual reunion when former members of one battalion brawl with those of another in the streets and pubs of the town. The army itself plays no part in the political life of the constituency. The officers and their wives may have registered to vote, but the bulk of the other ranks do not bother to do so. Nevertheless, there is a military flavour to the local Tories, so many of whom have, at one time, served in the British Army.

The Aldershot Tories may be poor but the Aldershot Conservative club is rich. The club is quite separate from the association, although the local party does have its office in the club building. I doubt if we could afford to rent a shop on our own. Conservative clubs are a political phenomenon to which too little attention has been paid. In Aldershot the club occupies a large building (*circa* 1933) in what has become a prime site in the middle of the town. Its subscription is low and, in consequence, its membership is high. It is, in effect, the town's club, providing bar facilities and entertainment far superior to the majority of the town's other 'pubs'. It is generally crowded. The bar is well stocked with fruit machines and the walls decorated with portraits of Winston Churchill and Mrs Thatcher. At elections the association will receive a generous donation to the Fighting Fund, but it would be an exaggeration to claim that the club is a powerhouse of Conservative party activity. It is not. Perhaps there is money in Aldershot, after all. Some years ago I was standing at the bar when a man I did not know approached me and thrust his wrist-watch beneath my nose. 'How much do you think I paid for this?' he demanded. I said I had no idea. 'Seven thousand pounds'.

Most people have some idea of what an MP does at Westminster but they have little idea of what he gets up to in the constituency. I suppose there must once have been a time when the Member paid his annual visit to the constituency, an occasion when he was met by a brass band at the railway station and paraded through the streets. Oliver Lyttelton devotes a paragraph only of his autobiography to 'Aldershot'. Edmund Burke, upon whom we Tories still rely for the distinction between a representative (which we are) and a delegate (which some would like us to be),

19

wrote, when his constituents reproached him with the rareness of his appearances in Bristol, 'But, gentlemen, I live a hundred miles distance from Bristol; and at the end of a session I come to my own house, fatigued in body and mind, to a little repose, and to a very little attention to my family and private concerns . . . I could hardly serve you as I have done, and court you too.'

Today we are perpetual suitors. Clement Attlee's Labour party invented the constituency 'surgery' where the MP invites the aggrieved to visit him with their complaints which are, more often than not, about the lack of a council house, a passport, or the dilatoriness, real or imagined, of the local office of the Department of Health and Social Security. The poorer the seat, the heavier the caseload. Visits to people and institutions are desirable things to do in themselves, but they are, at least, controllable. Newly elected MPs get invited everywhere. Eager beavers behave like minor royalty prompting invitations to schools, hospitals and bus depots, an exercise in self-publicity which I abandoned years ago. The unplanned visit can put busy people to a lot of unnecessary trouble. I simply make myself available to anyone who asks to see me.

An MP's diary will contain invitations to attend official functions held locally, such as Mayor-making and the opening of a new building or branch of a firm. Lunch with the Soroptimists or dinner with the General; Divine Service on Remembrance Day, and with it the parade where the Mayor takes the salute. In Aldershot the procession is led by a squad of Royal Military Policemen, mounted with lances, followed by a Para battalion, the Catering Corps, terrible with banners on which can be discerned the device 'Diner's Club', the Scouts and the Women's Royal Army Corps. Had I been Secretary of State for Defence I would have instituted two reforms for which I would have long been remembered: a ban on army bands playing in tents (or at dinner) and a ban on women soldiers marching. Everything goes in all directions. A sole elderly Canadian brings up the rear in Aldershot's November procession – the last survivor of the Canadians who rioted in 1945 and burnt down part of the centre of the town. Could he have been the man of the match?

The Aldershot Tories will do anything to raise an honest penny. A vacant shop in a run-down part of the town will be used as a 'second-hand shop' where items ranging from old typewriters to the entire wardrobes of the recently dead will be flogged off to the general public. The shop is staffed by Tory ladies. Three or four times a year in different parts of the constituency we will hold 'supper clubs' where the food is provided by one stalwart supporter and a visiting speaker is invited to round off the proceedings. In the past we have held dances or 'balls', usually to celebrate some great election victory. The most enjoyable was held at the Guildhall in Rochester after my surprise win in October 1959. We danced the night away to the sound of the 'Temperance Seven'. In Aldershot we move in a stately fashion, more becoming to those of us who have reached what Hartley Wintney calls 'the prime of life'. In place of a band playing New Orleans jazz, we swoop uncomfortably to the noise of three yobs and an amplifier.

We have, occasionally, been permitted by the Camberley Tories to join their annual dance at Lakeside, a nightclub built on the sands of Bagshot. These are grand affairs which are attended by a thousand people (twenty from Aldershot) where a stand-up comedian tells filthy jokes, the local MPs draw the raffle, and after an unmemorable dinner of tepid chicken, tinned peaches and cream, and Yugoslav hock, we take to the floor. If anyone ever doubted that politics is essentially a vulgar activity, the Tory Ball at Lakeside would set their minds at rest.

The annual dinner (no dance) is the principal function of the year. It is my task to persuade a prominent Conservative politician to be its guest of honour. We have listened respectfully to a series of 'great men': Michael Heseltine (when he was hard to get), Edward Heath, Jim Prior, Cecil Parkinson (when he was freely available), John Moore and John Major. I forget the rest. The fact that I have been able to persuade so many of my contemporaries to make the eighty-mile round trip, has been a source of pleasure, and surprise, to my local party. I am in their debt.

What is it that makes us accept an invitation to speak in someone else's constituency? Is it vanity? Gratitude for a previous appearance on the part of a friend in one's own? Or simply inertia, the inability to say 'no'? I suppose the real reason is that we all have the need to take in each others' washing. I hurry to say that I am not greatly in demand. Even were I a 'true believer' in word and deed, a dedicated foot-soldier in Mrs Thatcher's counter-revolution, I am not much of a hand at exhortation. And exhortation is the order of the day. 'Onwards and upwards', those twenty-minute harangues so beloved by partisans of all shades, are not my forte. And doubt and mockery are not greatly in demand. Nevertheless, I do top the bill from time to time, quitting Aldershot for richer pastures, speaking not in draughty village halls but in the converted barns of lovely homes in the Weald of Kent where 'new' money jostles the old, and the Jaguars, Porsches and BMWs clutter up the gravelled drives.

In return for a performance in or around Aldershot, I perform in dinner jacket to an audience of the mid-Surrey middle class: fifty or so couples who have paid £15 a head. It gives me a chance to see how the other half lives. The reception committee is female as is perhaps to be expected in a party which is run by one woman and sustained in office by the feet of many others. Conservative associations are suffering from what has come to be known as 'the flight of the men'; the disappearance of husbands who are too busy making their pile to play politics, and their replacement by their indomitable wives. But then Tory women are generally to be preferred to Tory men.

I do find these dinners something of an ordeal. I suppose all performers, whether actors, dons or parsons, want to get their part in the proceedings over quickly, and can only relax once they have sung and danced. Tory dinners in Thatcher's England start with sherry and build slowly to a climax, a succession of dishes served by harrassed waitresses: fish paté, beef stew with the inevitable rice, and lemon mousse, spiced with forced conversation with one's neighbours. There can only be so much to be said about Marbella. But here I have often struck lucky. In the northern suburbs of London at an annual dinner and dance where an elderly man in fancy dress played the organ throughout the meal, lost in an erotic reverie I sat next to a woman with whom I had danced in the Festival Ballet in Oxford nearly forty years ago. She had been a professional dancer. I had signed up as an extra in *Scheherazade* for three nights at ten bob a night. After the Nescafé, the prima ballerina and I solemnly opened the dancing.

Some of these formidable women do have views. I was greeted by the woman chairman of a constituency which bears the name of a Sussex new town with the words 'When I started reading *Westminster Blues* I didn't much like you . . . when I finished it I still didn't like you' – as good an example of a political hard knock as you will find. And there is the problem of how much to drink. Sir Oswald Mosley in his autobiography advised politicians to eschew alcohol. 'Rely', he said sternly, 'on your natural adrenalin to see you through,' Oh God that I could. We should never forget the iron law of public speaking. One glass of Mouton Cadet is enough: each additional glass equals an extra ten minutes of oratory. The speaker should rise sober. The fact that his audience will be drunk should work to his advantage.

Do cabinet ministers accept promotion on the understanding that part of their duty is to travel the country speaking at dinners as a favour to the more humble members of their party? I would certainly be discouraged by any such stipulation. The hurried clamber into a shabby dinner jacket, the long drive to an unmarked hall, the steady munching of the party faithful, the furtive glance at one's illegible notes, the scattered applause once you have been finally delivered and the long trail back to bed is a high price to pay for a battered red box. Yet whatever the quality of our performance, we should never forget that the Tory party is not at its best on its feet.

The choice of a guest speaker at the annual dinner does present an MP with a pretty problem. We are judged, not by the quality of our own contributions, which are usually limited to a vote of thanks, but by the quality of the guest speaker. In Aldershot we hold our annual dinner at the Officers' Club, seated in the ballroom where Miss Joan Hunter Dunn might once have danced the night away in the arms of a subaltern. Cabinet ministers in full flood have been known, somewhat disconcertingly, to bounce gently up and down, standing as they do upon the best-sprung dance floor in Europe. The guest is briefly introduced. He makes a charming speech in which he is nice about the local MP ('a good egg') and then permits questions which can range from the serious to the not so grave ('When will our MP get a job?'). He is then whipped off to the station to catch a train which will bring him exhausted back to London at midnight. The Aldershot

Tories, who will have dined on the Roast Beef of Old England, and drunk the wines of Spain, draw the raffle and happily go home.

There are risks involved on the part of the local MP. A cabinet minister in his prime, privy to official secrets and with the habit of referring to the Great Ones of our party by their Christian names, can put the MP in the shade; a mere pedestrian at the side of so sleek a Rover. The choice of a promising young backbencher can be even more hazardous. He will be fluent, passionate and sincere, and will hold strong views on all the topics you would rather not have aired. The wisest course, perhaps, is to invite backbenchers even older, less articulate and less distinguished than oneself. But such MPs are greatly in demand. The best tactic was surely that of another Hampshire MP who took great care to invite no colleague on to his patch. 'If I am to stand comparison,' he once proclaimed, 'let it be with the Mayor.' Even so I bet he drew the raffle.

The local Conservative party is an undemanding animal. We Tories are still, if only just, the non-political political party. Views are still left to the Member. One quality that the MP must possess is that of disguising the less agreeable side of his nature. What is called for is ordinary politeness and a gift for concealing boredom. A sense of humour is not essential (Mrs Thatcher has not got one) but it does help at your third Bring and Buy. Good humour and a capacity for relating names to faces are qualities which, when found in an MP's wife, can save a marriage. Be charming and be on time. Do not hogg the conversation: grave attention is the best antidote to poisonous rubbish. If you become a minister and rise in the political world it will be taken as a compliment to your supporters for it was they who had the good sense to choose you as their candidate in the first place. If you stay on the backbenches, well and good. If you want to kick over the political traces, as I have done, then you must work harder in the constituency. It is more important to be liked than admired. After a meeting in which there had been adverse criticism of something I had said or written, I overheard one member of the executive committee say to another, 'Well, at least he has put us on the map'. There are worse epitaphs.

24

# 3

# The Women in His Life

BENJAMIN DISRAELI'S reputation may not have survived Lord Blake's magisterial biography, but he is still remembered by Tories with affection. This is not so much on account of his espousal of the concept of 'One Nation', 'Thatcherism' having, according to Mrs Thatcher herself, 'changed everything', but because of his dictum that 'only married men were regular attenders at the House of Commons.' He was as right about that as he was about the need for the Tory party's appeal to be directed to all classes of society. But to return to the place of women in British politics. The Palace of Westminster is no pleasure dome; it is, quite simply, a refuge from domesticity.

Every evening just before 7 o'clock, a chorus of Tory MPs gathers outside the doors of the Members' Dining Room, waiting to take a regular place at table – Mr Wyn Roberts, Mr Robin Maxwell-Hyslop, Sir Trevor Skeet, Sir Paul Dean and Sir Michael Shaw – proof, if ever it were needed, of the proposition that, despite everything, the House of Commons is still a gentlemen's club.

The Tory party has only reluctantly adjusted to the arrival of women at Westminster. Women in politics, with the possible exception of the young Barbara Castle, have been granted the status of honorary men. The arrival of yet another stout party from the shires, wearing sensible shoes, is likely to be remarked on over the Brown Windsor soup without enthusiasm. But then we Tories have always been great deplorers: the Great Reform Bill, the coming of the railways and Lloyd George's budget were events out of which no good could reasonably be expected to come. Many a grey head was shaken on Mrs Thatcher's election to the leadership of the Conservative party in 1975 in the so-called 'Peasants' Revolt'.

Even today, putting Mrs Thatcher on one side, which is admittedly not easily done, the male MP has put women in their place. His arrival at midday on a Monday after a weekend spent at home is met by the murmured greetings of deferential policemen. His coat is taken from him by a male attendant. The Members' Lobby is staffed by one-time members of the SAS, dressed as penguins, from whom MPS receive telephone messages written out on pink slips, and the post office is staffed solely by men. Even the lobby correspondents who stand about sucking the ends of their pencils all wear trousers. The misogynist Member can, if he avoids both the tea room and the library where lurk pretty girls with degrees, arrive safely at his room beneath the eaves to which he will eventually summon his secretary.

There are at least three women in a politician's life: his wife, his secretary and his researcher. The last is an optional extra. MPS' wives, who we were told in the 'sixties review 'Beyond the Fringe' 'lead such solitary lives', surface publicly only in times of tribulation. When prominent politicians come a cropper, ensnared, more often than not, by their secretaries, their wives appear bravely on television, giving their errant husbands the benefit of the doubt. Mary Archer came out of the Archer affair with some of the credit previously gained by Anne Parkinson. Otherwise an MP's wife lives quietly at home in or near the constituency, pregnant if still young, opening fêtes and pouring coffee. Little wonder that sooner or later, so many of them bolt.

The Member's wife plays an important role if her husband is a Conservative. She will, as we have seen, have been scrutinised at the time of her husband's selection as prospective parliamentary candidate – summoned to say a few words – and cast by a panel of party activists as an elegant substitute before whom no raffle will remain undrawn and no bazaar unvisited.

The Labour party, on the other hand, shows little interest in the wives of parliamentarians. What Labour MPS do with their private lives is deemed by the Labour party (although not the gutter press) to be their own business. Labour wives are not expected to stand publicly at the side of their spouses. Unless they are as politically committed as their husbands, they stay at home. And Labour constituency parties are far less social than their Tory counterparts.

The Tory wife may well devote her weekends to several constituency engagements of a routine kind: the supper club with its visiting speaker, the Summer Fayre and the Coffee Morning, only to wave farewell to her husband who leaves the nest at dawn at the wheel of his second-hand Rover (the favourite motor-car of MPS, large, fast and comfortable, and affordable thanks to a mileage allowance for cars over 2,000cc of nearly 56 pence a mile), bound for Westminster and the other two women in his life. 'Back on Friday for a "bring and buy"' can be a message of no consolation.

The popular press has created the myth of the MP's secretary and researcher. Ms Pamella Bordes has much to answer for. If the tabloids are to be believed, the Palace of Westminster is not so much a talking as a knocking shop, where politicians with time on their hands, and twenty thousand pounds to spend on 'secretarial assistance', pass their time in dalliance. Like all legends it contains a grain of truth, but it is one which has become sadly exaggerated in recent years.

It is true that secretaries have been known to marry MPS (mine married John Biffen), but their nubility has been much magnified. Those secretaries with whom I sometimes stand in line to collect my post in the early morning in the Members' Lobby seem thoroughly respectable. When the House sits at 2.30 p.m., they are driven like money-changers from the Members' Lobby to make room for wives and mothers. Tory MPS do tend to employ girls called Fiona with piercing Petersfield accents, whose green wellies and Harrods bags can be glimpsed beneath their desks in the Norman Shaw building, which was once Scotland Yard and is now dignified with MPS' offices. And, I am sorry to say, the younger the MP, the younger his secretary.

Labour MPS whose values are more Victorian sometimes employ the little woman as their secretary, which keeps her salary in the family and helps to secure the marital bond. As keeper of her husband's daily diary, she, at least, can claim to know where he is. Whatever the relationship may be between employer and employed, there are no secrets from the corps of Members' secretaries, who can be relied on to be the first to know the worst, and to pass it on swiftly, if only to each other.

After the abandoned wife and the dutiful secretary, who if she is any good not only types but also writes the letters, comes the researcher. I have had several over the years: a nonagenarian Catholic theologian, a former features editor of a great newspaper, and more than one pretty American 'intern'. Indeed, researchers are often Americans from one of the smarter colleges who have persuaded their doting parents that six months passed in London working for an MP will help with grades. The girls are pretty but not much use. No sooner have they discovered that MPs are not Congressmen than their time is up: MPs who have wracked their brains to find something for them to do are in the end relieved to see them off.

The Tories may have elected a woman leader but the Whips' Office recruits only from among the gentlemen of the party. There has never been a woman whip. Who can tell whether such obvious discrimination is based upon class or upon sex? The Tory whips are very largely drawn from the diminished ranks of eldest sons, or from the Purple of Commerce, and are believed as a group to be no admirers of Mrs Thatcher. Given a common room to themselves, and under instructions to turn the lights out before leaving, the Tory whips have made themselves at home. The place smells of the changing-rooms of Eton. Muddy shirts and shorts are tossed over the backs of chairs; *The Sporting Life* is strewn upon the floor; and unwashed whisky glasses abound. Most whips keep whippets, and long afternoons are passed with the help of squash. The walls of the common room are hung with sporting prints, while the corridor leading to the Chief Whip's Office is lined with Etty's erotica. The Tory Whips' Office is to the equality of the sexes what the Bastille was to the French Revolution.

MPs may seek a refuge from domesticity but we have more than our fair share of vanity. We tend to preen as well as posture. If we are in love it is usually with ourselves. Perhaps MPs are not as potent as the gutter press would have us believe? To disguise our self-absorption, we encourage a few of our number to write fiction in which the hero is a randy Tribune, the heroine his blonde secretary, and the victim his mousy wife. The action takes place before the backdrop of Westminster. Maurice Edelman wrote winningly about 'fifties fornication in novels in which no minister of the crown was without his mistress. David Walder wrote of love among the Young Conservatives, cheerful tennis-playing girls in Aertex shirts, and Wilfred Fienburgh claimed there was no love for Johnnie. Even Denis Potter, a politician manqué, has done as much for Nigel Barton. There is even, or so I have been told, a little love in Jeffrey Archer.

If only it all were true. The Palace of Westminster, with its thousand rooms, its secret staircases of the sort employed by cardinals at Frascati to visit their amorata, its deserted corridors leading, as in di Lampedusa's summer palace at Donnafugata, to forgotten rooms furnished with the instruments of vice, could be a Temple to Venus. We would, however, be continually inter-rupted by the ringing of bells, bells which would summon us, like so many Betjemans, to do our duty in the division lobby. When it was decided in the 'sixties by Harold Wilson that MPs should have free postage, secretaries and a room of their own, it was also decided that, unlike the Chambre des Députés, we should be given a desk, chair and telephone, but never a bed. England remains at heart a Protestant country.

It will not take the newcomer to Westminster long to recognise the fact that MPs are overwhelmingly white, male and middle-class. This is true of all the parties. There are no black Tories but many who are red-necked. There are usually more Labour women MPs than there are Tories, but only the Conservative party would wish to claim Margaret Hilda Thatcher as its own. The Tory party has come down in the world as the Labour party has gone up, but the end result remains the same. The attitudes of MPs towards women are little or no different from those of any other group of middle-class males. If anything we are more liberal. It has not been MPs who have kept women out of Westminster but the small committees of the self-selected in the constituencies. And it is the majority of women members of those committees who have conspired to exclude members of their own sex from becoming candidates. Wherever else a woman's place may be, it is not yet at Westminster. The vote of no confidence in women politicians has been passed not by men, but by women.

In the event, the male dominance of the Palace of Westminster remains unchallenged. There is, it is true, a woman policeman who takes her turn in the box under the awning where MPs queue for taxis in New Palace Yard, but the rest of the force is stolidly male. Women MPs have no place in Mrs Thatcher's rapidly changing cabinets. They are allocated lavatories and changing-rooms of their own: otherwise we are permitted to live a monastic life into which we allow some rain to fall in the guise of secretarial assistance. Perhaps we really are male chauvinist pigs waited on hand and foot. Once a day our secretaries bring us our letters to sign: jolly Irish waitresses serve us our portion of Cabinet Pudding; and clever girls in the library ask us to sign for copies of the *Gentleman's Magazine*. Protected from our wives (and mothers), to say nothing of the public at large, by a hand-picked force of the Metropolitan police, we are free to escape into the Smoking Room and ask George to open a bottle of champagne. The odds on being joined by the Prime Minister are 360 to 1.

I think it was Sir Jocelyn Lucas who told me one evening at dinner that the two occupational risks of an MP were alcohol and adultery. 'The Lords', he said sternly, 'has the cup for adultery'. Lucas, who was a nice old thing who bred Sealyhams, lived a blameless life, but there have been others who have been less fortunate. There have been at intervals, a haroosh; a newspaper-inspired fuss in which the British are encouraged to indulge themselves in a display of hypocrisy (surely, our favourite Victorian 'virtue'?), a warming of hands before the revelation that some public figure has been caught by the editor of the *Sun* newspaper with his trousers around his ankles in what will be called a love-nest. I have lived through many such episodes: the Profumo affair which helped to bring down Harold Macmillan; the Parkinson affair which gave all, save for its principals, as much gratuitous pleasure as winning the World Cup; and a host of minor episodes featuring such tyros as Lord Lambton. The saga of Ms Bordes's life and loves is but the latest. Others have been luckier. The Palace of Westminster has a thousand rooms, but not a thousand keyholes.

Whether or not MPs are much-married, happily or unhappily married, uxorious or fancy-free, we do enjoy the opportunity to philander. By the same token, the fact that the bars stay open into the long reaches of the night offers temptation to which many have succumbed. Not every adulterer is an alcoholic, or vice versa: all I am asserting is that MPs, by the nature of their job, have the opportunity to kick over the traces, an opportunity denied to many a nine-to-fiver, and shared with sea captains, commercial travellers and airline pilots. An MP with two houses – one in or near the constituency, the other a studio flat in Lambeth – can enjoy a cooked breakfast in both. The fact that the majority of us live blameless lives can be put down either to virtue or to fatigue.

It has been asserted often enough that MPs have the highest divorce rate of any occupation, although I have never been shown the evidence for it. I would not be surprised if it were almost true. By its nature, politics is a calling where admiration plays an important part. We loved to be loved. No MP courts universal unpopularity and most take care to retain the affection, or at the very least the respect, of their party activists. We perform, and as performers thrive upon applause.

Wives can be the antidote to vanity, but they play their part as the candid friend at no little risk to themselves. A husband who is to all intents and purposes a 'weekly boarder' can return to a bored wife who has come to dislike 'politics' and all that is implied by it. An MP cannot pick his friends. In the constituency they pick themselves from among the self-selected, the zealots who, untypically, take the trouble to join a political party. Even in the Tory party, the MP's 'parson's freehold' cannot be taken for granted. The MP can be reminded by party agent or party chairman that he is at Westminster on sufferance, that it is the party that adopts, and, more significantly, re-adopts, the parliamentary candidate. It is sometimes from among the ranks of the censorious that the MP's 'friends' can be drawn.

Not all wives live in exile in Eatanswill West; some follow their husbands to London, returning with them to their constituencies at weekends; but many, burdened with small children, and comparatively hard up, stay put. The arrival of their husbands late on a Friday night (having spoken at a party meeting that evening on their return from Westminster) dumb with exhaustion, can poison the atmosphere. Saturdays spent opening bazaars and then dining with the local Rotary Club do little to improve relations. At least Sunday may be a day of rest. The abandoned wife is at a further disadvantage. She lives a humdrum life; her husband sits at the centre of events. He may play little or no active part in them but he is a spectator, the owner of a ringside seat. And the MP's week can be enlivened by invitations: drinks with the Mexican ambassador; lunch with some lobbyist at the Terrace Room at the Dorchester Hotel or a speech to a colleague's constituency dinner in the House of Commons. Viewed from a house on the borders of Wales, the husband's life ('and, as I said to Margaret ...') can appear to be a pleasure-progress, an ego trip, a gentle round of events where late to bed can be compensated for by late to rise.

Cynics may claim that MPS are rotten lovers anyway, being in love with themselves. But that cannot apply to us all. If MPS are rotten lovers, the reason is more likely to be fatigue than vanity. The hours are anti-social, ridiculously so. Unless one is 'paired', the House, which meets at 2.30 p.m., can go on until 10 o'clock in the evening, and frequently well beyond it. Most MPS do two jobs, devoting the morning to making money, and the afternoon to politics. Ministers who work hard during the day are obliged to become 'backbenchers' in the evening, summoned to vote the ticket however hectic their day may have been. Speech-making, especially if it is in the House in an important debate, or answering parliamentary questions, can drain away one's nervous energy, the 'high' which follows the end of a successful speech being all too often followed by a 'low' for which bed is the only cure.

Bed, that is, or alcohol. As we age so the need for stimulants grows. At 30 I could sail through the discomforts of an all-night sitting, cat-napping in the library, chatting to my friends. I could even face a hearty breakfast, a feast which was once provided by the kitchens, but no longer. In my fifties I cannot bear the prospect of a night of discomfort after which I will feel like a traveller who has gone from Calais to Cannes overnight in a third-class carriage. I have no wish to feel dreadful for the whole of the next day. I find my 'pair', Eric Heffer, and we both push off, after 10 p.m., cancelling each other out by our absence. If I cannot find him, or if he wishes to take part in the debate, I go anyway. It is for the newly elected 'Thatcherites' in our party to hold the bridge, an exercise in which I have taken part, with more enthusiasm than I would show today, for the past twenty years.

The need for a drink to blunt fatigue or to banish boredom is increasingly hard to resist. Many MPS will take a gin or two before dinner, drink at least a half bottle of wine at table, and return to the Smoking Room, or Annie's or the Strangers' Bar or wherever, and, with the help of brandy, pass the night away. The wind-up between nine and ten o'clock, when the rival party middleweights exchange insults, can attract the cheerfully disposed from the Smoking Room into the Chamber, but not for long. If the House adjourns at ten, we drive home, despite the strictures of Mr Peter Bottomley: if it continues long into the night, many of us return to the bars for solace and for conversation. Work should be the alternative to dissipation. However, many people find the Palace a difficult place within which to work, and others who are at their best early in the morning cannot summon up the will-power necessary to read and write at midnight. It has long been the convention of the Commons that no Hon. Member can be 'drunk', and it is as well that we have the rule. Obvious drunkenness is rare, but the MP who goes home entirely sober is rarer still.

If MPS live by the press they can as easily perish by it. In the United States the private lives of politicians are fair game. Whereas twenty years ago President Kennedy's love life was kept out of the newspapers, today no politician's past or present is safe from exposure. Watergate is a possible explanation. Another is the reaction against the so-called 'permissive society', the chief spokesmen being members of the 'moral majority' whose influence within the Republican party is considerable despite the money-grubbing tactics of the born-again fundamentalists and the frequency with which the Swaggarts of this world are unmasked. A more obvious explanation might be that most of us enjoy reading about the downfall of the great and famous, their embarrassment being our pleasure. In Britain the rules have also changed. In the past the proprietors of our newspapers sought political careers of their own, and took care not to offend their peers unnecessarily. Today, the gutter press is largely foreign-owned.

In Britain, MPS are regarded as fair game. What is even worse is the tendency of the tabloids to go beyond the celebrity in search of copy. The *News of the World*, Mr Murdoch's flagship, devoted its centre page spread last summer to a story which it had got from the boyfriend of the daughter of a Tory MP. The girl had been on soft drugs; her boyfriend had been an addict. The story, which had no merit whatsoever, was illustrated by a photograph of Mr Patrick McNair Wilson MP and his wife, and the page was given what 'charge' it possessed by making the link between a 'senior' politician and his errant daughter. It was as nasty an example of gutter journalism as one could find. MPS are public men, and by becoming so do forfeit some, at least, of their privacy: the children of MPS are not public people. I mention this unsavoury piece of journalism only as a warning. If an MP's child takes to drink or drugs, or sleeps around, he or she is fair game for the likes of Ms Wendy Henry, then First Lady of the *News of the World*.

The only safe pleasure for a politician is a bag of boiled sweets.

# 4

# The Longest
# Day

WHENEVER I am asked what it is I do and I reply with some diffidence that I am an MP ('for my sins') the inference is that I work terribly hard. There are times when I do, although I suspect that my activities can be better described as energetic rather than industrious. Most people have not the slightest idea what MPs actually do. The belief that we sit all day in the Chamber engrossed by the speeches of our peers, rising to make a pithy contribution, or at the very least bellowing out 'hear, hear', is widespread, even among party activists who should know better. Visitors to the Commons gallery are invariably shocked when they see how small is the number of MPs in the Chamber. Where are they all? is their plaintive cry.

I shall attempt to describe a day in the life of a Conservative MP. I have chosen to write about Tories for reasons that are obvious; I am not too clear as to how the other half lives. On a normal day MPs will start to arrive at about 10 o'clock in the morning. Even after twenty-five years in the House I can still derive a certain pleasure from driving into New Palace Yard in my second-hand Rover 825SI (I have always bought British), past the tactful scrutiny of deferential policemen, then to pause while two uniformed men with mirrors on the end of sticks examine the underside of the car for Semtex. Then the plunge down into the underground car park with its five concrete floors searching for a place to park. (The 'fifth circle' is reserved, as Dante would have wished, for MPs' secretaries.) Free parking in central London, together with a valet service at £3 a motor-car, is one of the great advantages of being an MP. It can be difficult, however, to find a space. Some MPs use the garage as a warehouse; Sir

Frederic Bennett's Rolls-Royce spent years on bricks and Mr Alan Clark's gangster's motor (a 'fifties Chevvy?) jostled for the position of 'Father' of the Commons' garage.

The first-comers are MPS who have been put on committees of one sort or another which start at 10.30 a.m. These are of two kinds: select committees which were they racehorses might be described as being by Richard Crossman out of Norman St John-Stevas. They take a particular area of interest and study it in depth. Membership is decided not by the party whips but by backbench MPS of all parties: in the Tory party Sir Marcus Fox, the Conservative MP for Shipley in Yorkshire, known to his friends as 'the last of the summer wine', places volunteers on what is hoped is the committee of their choice. It pays to be nice to Marcus. The environment committee is chaired by Sir Hugh Rossi, a former minister at the Department of the Environment; the defence committee by Colonel Michael Mates, the Tory MP for Hampshire East. The composition of the committees reflects the number of MPS belonging to all the political parties. Select committees, which owe their existence to the American experience, have been grafted on to a very different Westminster system. They produce reports, written by their clerks, which are frequently adversely critical of Government policy. Their proceedings are open to the press. Ministers and civil servants can be summoned to attend, although they need not do so. Edwina Currie stayed away after her resignation. The most famous of the select committee reports was that of the defence committee on the Westland affair. One would expect the reports to be debated on the floor of the House, but it is the government of the day that controls the parliamentary timetable. The more embarrassing reports will be published but they will not be given parliamentary time.

The other kind of committee scrutinises bills. After the second reading debate has been held (the first reading is a formality), the bill, if it is passed, is taken 'upstairs' into committee, where the legislation is examined carefully line by line, and clause by clause. MPS who are sufficiently interested in the subject of the bill to speak either for or against in the second reading debate are put on the committee, once again in proportion to the political strength of the parties. The bill will be steered through the committee by the minister and his parliamentary secretary; the opposition will field their two 'shadow ministers'.

The composition of the committee is not made up entirely of enthusiastic volunteers. The whips are obliged to appoint the unwilling, a chore which is usually given to the newly elected with their way to make in the world. In 1959, the Englishman Mr Peter Emery, then the Conservative MP for a Reading seat, was placed, much against his will, on the Scottish Grand Committee. Having turned up twice in full Highland dress hired from a theatrical costumier, an act which gave much offence to Scots of every political persuasion, Emery was released from service on the committee. It was a good wheeze, and the whips did not hold it against him. No such escape route offered itself to me when I was press-ganged on to the Pipelines Bill in the early 'sixties.

If a bill is relatively uncontroversial, its passage upstairs will be smooth. Two committee meetings a week for three weeks on a Tuesday and a Thursday morning from 10.30 a.m. to 1 p.m. will suffice. When the bill is controversial, the opposition will fight it 'line by line', calling a series of votes, and keeping the committee in session throughout the afternoon, and even throughout the night. When faced with so appalling a prospect, the only antidote to boredom and discomfort is to play a vigorous part in the committee's proceedings in the knowledge that in politics, as in Parliament, it is better to be busy than bored. Some of the most hectic parties have been held at the end of a frightful ordeal 'upstairs', the more generous whips, such as Sir Spencer Le Marchant, providing champagne and tasty bits. Even so, I would rather have stayed in bed.

The early shift having divested itself of coat, hat and sword (a loop is tactfully provided in the Members' cloakroom, on which one's weapon may be suspended), MPs make for the tea room via the Members' Post Office. The Post Office abuts on the Members' Lobby, a circus around which former Premiers stand on plinths. There are two vacant ones, both of which are reserved for Mrs Thatcher. Some MPs leave it to their secretaries to collect their letters. Others, menaced by the post, collect it themselves, and take it into the tea room where, over a cup of instant coffee, they open it. The practised eye skims over the pile of white, separating into a second heap the brown-enveloped second class, the majority of which can be tossed carelessly into a waiting bin. Magazines such as *The Concrete Quarterly* or the *Water Board Gazette* are swiftly dispatched, begging letters dismissed and round robins from colleagues ripped in half. The first-class mail is then divided into two: those which bear the postmark of the constituency and those which do not. Constituency mail is, in its turn, either supplicatory ('Would you be so good as to raise with the Minister of X the problem of my wife's invalidity benefit?') or condemnatory ('We note that you did not vote in favour of Mr Alton's bill on abortion and we take pleasure in telling you that we shall not vote for you when the next election comes round . . .'). The first is acted upon promptly; the second, briefly acknowledged. The rest of the whites can be divided into cheques, payment for an article written or an opinion expressed to camera, and letters from the world beyond Aldershot. Hate mail can result from controversial opinions expressed in tabloid newspapers. I once wrote a piece in the *Sun* suggesting that we should not bring back capital punishment for murder. For some days afterwards I received abuse in thin envelopes and two death threats, unsigned, from Manchester. Rude letters go unanswered: polite letters of appreciation receive a cheerful acknowledgement. I have always much enjoyed opening my letters, and I make sure that they follow me on holiday. The more sanguine MP delegates the task of letter-opening to his secretary, and is offered, once a day, a neat file in which rest only those which she considers to be worthy of his attention. The angry who rush to pen and ink and write letters of abuse might be saddened, if not discouraged, were they to be aware that the cutting phrase and the wounding retort never actually reach the eye of their victim. And our secretaries, who are usually youngish married women with broad backs, seem to be entirely unaffected by them. No doubt the riper correspondence is held back to show other secretaries who are not so fortunate in their Member.

I make a habit of always collecting my own post and opening it myself over a cup of painfully black coffee (19p) in the tea room. The tea room is a sequence of 'rooms' with a counter at one end. Labour MPs congregate immediately upon entry. Tories sit in the second room and the clerks and librarians make use of the far end. A bevy of cheerful girls, black and Irish, dispense pots of tea, toast, and, at lunch and supper time, plates of undistinguished pork pie of the sort that has an egg in the middle. In the mornings it becomes a meeting-place, where MPs *en route* to the committee room corridor read the newspapers (all of which are provided), open their post to exclamations of dismay ('another letter from that bloody lunatic') and indulge in that most favoured of topics; gossip about the standing of the great and not so great. Not every MP will rush upstairs at 10.29: others, of scholarly bent, may visit the library in order to obtain help from its staff in the writing of a speech, an article, or the tabling of a question. Still others will take the lifts to their offices under the eaves where they will make use of the free telephone in furtherance of their private affairs.

Nowadays nearly every MP has a room of his own. Ken Livingstone, the Labour MP for Brent, wandered the Palace of Westminster like a lost soul. If he was roomless it was because the Labour whip in charge of accommodation, who is known to his colleagues as 'Sugar' Ray Powell, was reluctant to find him one. As a senior backbencher I have had a room of my own for the past five years. It is simply furnished with two desks, a file, a glass-fronted cupboard and an armchair. It is cold in both summer and winter, needs a new coat of paint very badly indeed, and the Venetian blinds are filthy. I have stuck up the originals of political cartoons on my walls. Sir Patrick Wall used to hang model aircraft from the ceiling of his, and elsewhere there are Pirelli-type calendars, but the run of MPs' rooms have a simple quality. We are not a frivolous lot.

Tory MPs take luncheon. Or some of them still do. Newly elected Conservative MPs of a Thatcherite disposition tend to eat dinner at lunch or to have their supper for dinner in the tea room 'off a tray'. The sight of the Prime Minister's praetorian guard faced with a plate of corned beef salad on which rests a single undressed tomato, complaining about the amount of public subsidy to the arts, is not one for the squeamish. But, prompt upon the stroke of 1 o'clock, the Tory party proper moves into the Members' Dining Room from the Smoking Room and parcels itself out among the tables. There are perhaps half a dozen small tables which seat four, one of which is traditionally reserved for the Chief Whip. There are besides two large tables with room for nine. The Tories sit at the north end of the large room, next to the Smoking Room. The Liberals have a largish table to themselves in the middle, and the People's Party occupies the southern end, the end, that is, nearest to Jeffrey Archer's penthouse riverside flat.

Lunch is fun. Or it can be, for much depends upon the character of one's neighbour. We do have our bores. And, although it might be asserted that we all, whatever our capacity, stay on for a term, or a Parliament, too long, we are by no means always old. Westminster bores have a passion for re-counting at length the nature and extent of their ward boundaries, followed by the recital of their majorities at every election since 1959. Some have been known, flushed with the effect of a half bottle of Grant's of St James's 'house claret', to describe with daunting accuracy the political composition and make-up of their district council. Old bores are to be preferred to young ones. Their knowledge of the events and the personalities of the day before yesterday, those now forgotten but once 'great' names such as Ernest Marples, Mr Ray Mawby, Sir Harry Legge-Bourke and Sir Hugh Monroe Lucas-Tooth come alive again in all their glory. Lunch is better than dinner. The food seems fresher, and the cross-section of one's fellows larger and thus less predictable. Were I to choose a table of nine, and I shall do so at my peril, I would pick Nigel Lawson who is invariably entertaining, Nicholas Soames, the only Tory MP to wear five buttons on his cuff, Nicholas Budgen who is ignited by a single glass of plonk, St Michael Allison whose natural charity would act as an antidote to malice, Douglas Hogg who is as amusing as he is intelligent, Virginia Bottomley who would see to our manners, and Tristan Garel-Jones who knows everything. As eighth man I would pick Dr Alan Glyn upon whose legal advice we could rely in case of dispute, and whose medical expertise might, were the laughter to rise to too high a pitch, come in very handy. These are but nine, chosen at random: but I should warn that there are many others in our great party for whom the kiss of life has long been a necessity.

Tea is taken after questions. In the tea room, which accommodates the Tories at one end and Labour MPs at the other, girls pass out the buns (the Commons has long been notorious for its rock cakes which have a unique and alarming density), while the more sensitive take China tea and finger their copies of the *Evening Standard*. Here again the tables are large and can be a place of refuge for the minister and his team who have just been fielding the questions. Mr Norman Fowler has been known to pass through the length of the tea room looking for all the world as if he were an Anglican bishop, pausing to bless the tables in turn. Sometimes the Prime Minister herself has been known to take tea. Mrs Thatcher never moves beyond the Chamber without Mr Mark Lennox-Boyd in tow. Mark is her parliamentary private secretary. He will get the tea; a chorus of the newly elected will provide the sympathy. Older hands will mumble their apologies and slide away, for Mrs Thatcher's temper is as uncertain as her views are fixed. There is a piece to be written, although not by me, on the significance of Mrs Thatcher's apparel. To catch a glimpse of Mrs Thatcher *en route* to some conference hall or auditorium wearing a bright blue toque is to be certain that the nation is in for a well-deserved thrashing. She wears brick-red to receive Mr Gorbachev.

Dinner is perhaps a more sombre occasion than is luncheon. I used to dine with Sally Oppenheim-Barnes, a pretty woman who was, in her youth, a dancer. She eventually became a Dame (most Tory women MPS do). She almost invariably had a lobster and a half bottle of hock. The wine I did not covet, but I did the claw which for some unaccountable reason she invariably left on the side of her plate. The fact that Sally is Jewish did not account for her prejudice as the rest of the lobster was always eaten. Greatly daring, I once asked if I might finish her claw, after which we became firm friends. The advantage of dining early, especially on nights when there is a running whip and a vote at 10 o'clock, is the service. Dine after 8 and the place is packed and the service becomes harrassed. As the noise level rises, and with it the heat of a summer's evening, one can glimpse a curious British social custom. Sooner or later Labour MPS will remove their jackets and sit unabashedly in their shirt sleeves. Even Mrs Thatcher's Conservative party does no such thing. The sight of Tory MPS with sweat dripping into their beaujolais, caught in the straitjacket of a middle-class convention, is a faintly ridiculous one. In the summer of 1988, I came in to dine late in the company of Mr Austin Mitchell, the Labour MP, and Mr Charles Kennedy, the SDL MP. We had been recording a political quiz show for the BBC, and had determined, in the taxi, that we should defy convention and sit together. We sat at the Tory end. There was an almost imperceptible drop in the level of conversation. Mitchell and Kennedy removed their coats, and, as good manners dictated, so did I. The silence which greeted this gesture was first shocked; then it was succeeded by a round of applause. When in Rome. But no other Tory, despite the temperature, took off his jacket.

Every MP of whatever political party receives each Friday the Whip. This document, published by the respective Whips' Offices, announces the business in the House for the week to come. Mrs Thatcher's much-vaunted 'radicalism' has resulted in an increasingly heavy parliamentary work-load with long hours and shorter holidays. In 1959, Conservative Governments used to boast of the paucity of legislation – legislation being an activity much favoured by the Labour Movement. Today we are all on the treadmill of the counter-revolution.

A good day will be one on which there is a one-line whip which means that attendance is only 'requested'. That is usually the case on Fridays when the House sits from 9.30 a.m. to 2.30 p.m. and takes private as opposed to Government business. A two-line whip offers the opportunity of 'pairing' with a Labour MP. It is very much in the interest of all MPs to find a pair, a luxury which permits him to go home to his wife at a reasonably early hour. Eric Heffer, my pair, is a Christian-Socialist with a short fuse. His habit of addressing small groups of Marxists in draughty village halls means that he is quite often away – which makes him an ideal pair. A three-line whip means that pairing is not allowed. Since the 1987 election, when Labour did so poorly, the Labour whips have countered our two-liners with a three-liner of their own, a tactic designed to keep their noses to the grindstone but one which has the deplorable effect of nullifying our own relative generosity. Since a three-line whip means that the Member of Parliament cannot pair, if he is *in extremis*, he will have to visit the pairing-whip cap in hand, armed with a cock-and-bull story.

Ten o'clock in the evening is the watershed hour. The House

will begin at 2.30 p.m. with prayers, followed by an hour of questions. Unless there is a ministerial statement at 3.30 p.m., which will take up to an hour, depending upon its importance, the debate, which is the principal business of the day, will not begin until 3.30. The weekly Whip will give advance warning of particularly contentious legislation which will mean the suspension of the 10 o'clock rule, and the dreaded prospect of the business going on into the watches of the night. Late nights are the bane of parliamentary life. In a rational world we would start proceedings in the morning and end them in the early evening, but since when has politics been a rational activity? MPs are paid as half-timers; the late start, and later hours permitting Members of Parliament to do several jobs, devoting the morning and most of the afternoon to their private affairs. Full-time MPs would demand a larger salary than their present one, and I have no doubt that the public, whose view of politicians veers from contempt to admiration and back again, would begrudge us an extra penny.

I have dwelt on the delights of lunching and dining with 'the colleagues'. Lunch plays an important part in the life of an MP. He will either take pot-luck in the Members' Dining Room, or respond to an invitation of his own, rashly made in the past, to a constituent or a friend to lunch with him at the House. I have often sat in the Central Lobby waiting for my guests, and have watched the arrival of other MPs, who leaving the Members' Lobby with a fixed, even grave expression upon their faces, suddenly break into delighted smiles at the sight of their constituency chairman. Any casual visitor to London with time on his hands could do far worse than come into the Central Lobby (the trick is to give the name of an MP, any MP, to the security staff), take a seat and watch the world go by. It is warm and dry.

The Central Lobby is never empty. Elderly, even decrepit, peers will emerge from the direction of the Lords, only to vanish as suddenly. Famous faces ('Look, that must be Norman Tebbit.') whisper to the attendants on the desk who promptly call out the names of the fortunate visitors. Giants from the past, like Lord Home, can be spotted striding briskly in the direction of the terrace. Pretty women arrive and leave promptly with an Hon. Member in tow, batches of earnest Americans gaze heavenward at the extravagant ceiling, the decoration of which, as is the case

43

with all of Pugin's work, is characterised by what contemporary economists call 'a high labour content'. There is a post office handy, and an attendant who, if asked nicely, will direct the visitor to a canteen downstairs where he can drink tea in the company of Mr Denis Healey. An elderly aunt of mine from the wilds of Shropshire, down in London for the day, sat in the Central Lobby for half an hour while I was held up in traffic. 'It were as good as a play' was her cheerful comment.

Lunch for constituents does not end with paying the bill. They are dutifully escorted to the Central Lobby in time for the Speaker's procession at 1.35 p.m. The Speaker and his chaplain, together with sundry flunkies, process with all the aplomb of a ceremony the roots of which must surely go back into the mists of time. In fact, the Speaker's procession was instituted after the last war, an act of genius, worthy of Mr Thomas Cook himself. The process marks the start of the day's business in the House: the MP with guests must now take them up into the Strangers' Gallery, having, with huge difficulty, procured beforehand the necessary tickets. Prime Minister's Questions, which are held from 3.15 to 3.30 on Tuesdays and Thursdays, are the main attraction. Mrs Thatcher's reputation has travelled abroad, and distinguished American visitors importune the American embassy for tickets.

The MP will say farewell to his guests with a feeling of relief and then hurry downstairs to take his place in the House for Question Time. Attendance is not obligatory; he is as likely to retire upstairs to his room and put his feet up for half an hour. A siesta is one way of successfully getting through the parliamentary day. Parliamentary Question Time is commonly regarded as the 'jewel' in the British Parliament's crown. It is, at first sight at least, remarkable enough that such important people as Ministers of the Crown should allow themselves to be cross-questioned by Members of Parliament and to do so in public. Political scientists talk admiringly of 'accountability'.

The 'game' is played to these rules: an MP will table a question, days in advance. That question ('Will the Prime Minister state her engagements for Thursday 4 July?') is replied to by Mrs Thatcher with a factual answer. 'In the morning I had an audience with Her Majesty the Queen; in the afternoon various meetings with Ministers . . .' The MP is then permitted a second bite, the thrust of which will be unknown to the Prime Minister. The quality of her reply will depend on the amount of homework done by her Downing Street office and herself. All possible 'supplementaries' will have to be covered. The second bite could cover anything from the price of eggs or mortgage tax relief to the likelihood of a 'summit' meeting or the date of the next general election. What fun (or information) there is to be derived from the whole exercise comes out of this cut and thrust. Each Ministry answers questions in turn to a published timetable. The Prime Minister does so for fifteen minutes twice a week.

The art of answering parliamentary questions can be acquired. What is needed on the part of a minister is wit, quick thinking and an adequate brief. Practice can make perfect. A minister who made a frequent hash of Question Time would be an embarrassment to the Government. His discomfiture would encourage the Opposition and humiliate the Government side. And the press, who are in the gallery for Question Time in strength, would make a meal of the minister's humiliation. It is very rare that a minister is unable to cope. The name of the game is party advantage. Question Time is the battlefield over which the Opposition and Government contend, the one determined to find some loophole, force some error: the other to defend its record and protect its rear. It can be theatre, but it is more likely to be dull and predictable.

MPs can make use of Question Time in various ways. Like cocks displaying in the hen-yard, we will table questions designed to embarrass the other side, defend our own, or even, quite simply, to elicit information. The Opposition backbench MP can use Question Time to skirmish in front of his front bench infantry; the Government backbencher is more likely to rise in order to make a supplementary which will be judged helpful to a minister. With an eye on the *Aldershot Bugle*, an MP will ask a question pertaining to a matter of local importance such as the closure of a hospital, or the opening of a new stretch of road. MPs as they rise are most often ignored by their fellows who keep up a running conversation with their neighbours.

Characters, such as Geoffrey Dickens, the 20-stone one-time amateur heavyweight boxer (he once went nine rounds with Don Cockell), are greeted with hoots of cheerful derision: earnest

45

Tory backbenchers who try to come to the aid of party and Premier are welcomed by the Opposition with Bronx cheers, party loyalists are met with raucous cries of 'Give 'im a job'. Dennis Skinner, the Beast of Bolsover (who would not hurt a fly unless it were stationary), keeps up a rumble of comment from a sedentary position. The rival backbenches below the gangway swop abuse, and, his voice rising indignantly above the bedlam, the Speaker appeals desperately for order. The broadcasting of questions on radio has come as a grave shock to the more sensitive of our citizens. We do not behave well, but it should be borne in mind by the more genteel that Parliament in the early afternoon is not the Council of the Nation; it is a cockpit, a substitute for violence. With the parties drawn up in lines of battle, an insult is to be preferred to a punch on the nose.

Spectators in the gallery come to see the duel between Mrs Thatcher and Mr Kinnock. Neil orates, while Margaret bellows. All Prime Ministers get the better of Leaders of the Opposition; they are the better briefed. Mrs Thatcher is not often caught out, but when in difficulty she shouts; lacking the humorous touch she finds it hard to defuse a tricky situation. Neil Kinnock is passionate but he can be garrulous and diffuse. More recently, he has begun to bowl her length. John Biffen, when he was Leader of the House and 'detached' from his leader, proved to be a most skilful performer when substituting for the Prime Minister. He had a light touch and was not afraid to play to the gallery. John Wakeham, Biffen's successor, is more pedestrian. It was he who told us that the reason for Mrs Thatcher's absence was because she was 'making herself available' to Mr Gorbachev. Ted Heath was never caught out; Harold Wilson was fly; James Callaghan almost always got the better of Mrs Thatcher; Alec Douglas Home was decent; Hugh Gaitskell was intense; and Harold Macmillan was elegant and witty.

The drama can continue beyond Question Time into a ministerial statement which is a continuation of all that has gone before but with a stated theme and a different cast. Ministers can be asked Private Notice Questions which oblige them to come down to the House to explain or defend themselves; for example Paul Channon over the Clapham railway disaster in December 1988. At the end of Question Time at 3.30 p.m. the Chamber empties, and MPS head for the tea room. There is a buzz of conversation and a great deal of what passes for good-natured badinage.

Refreshed by a cup of tea and the latest Edwina/Margaret/Michael story, the conscientious MP has a variety of tasks on offer. He might summon his Commons secretary to attend him in his room to take dictation, or to bring the letters written the day before for his signature. Harold Macmillan once said that the only quality needed to be an MP was the ability to write a good letter. An MP's post will wax and wane; in normal times I will get three or four letters a day from constituents. The burden becomes much heavier when there is a controversial issue before Parliament. Abortion, or the restoration of capital punishment, encourages a flood of mail. Generally, MPS are robust in the face of lobbyists pedalling views with which they disagree. I believe in the need for abortion, and do not favour the return of the rope. But the success of the Sabbatarian lobby in resisting the Government's intention to liberalise Sunday trading, shows how effective such a campaign can be. MPS like to live as quietly as possible, and we are sensitive to local pressures in particular. Moral matters present the greatest difficulty. MPS are not bishops, we are party hacks, and the party's policy does serve as a protection of sorts. But the parties take care to have no policy as such on what are called 'matters of conscience'. We are left very much on our own.

An MP may equally forego the pleasures of dictation, and return to the Chamber itself either to attempt to speak in the debate, or to listen to the proceedings. A standard debate, say on the second reading of a bill, will last from 3.30 to 10 o'clock. It will be opened and closed by thirty-minute speeches from the two front benches, with the spokesmen for the third and fourth parties called to speak after the Labour party and the Government have had their turn. Two and a half hours are thus taken out of the debate. Four and a half hours are left to backbenchers of all parties. Given a speech lasting fifteen minutes, there is room for eighteen other 'fifteen-minute' speeches, seven Tories, seven Labour and four odds and sods. Bearing in mind that there are 250 Tory backbenchers, it takes no great mathematical skill to see just how hard it is for an MP to catch the Speaker's eye.

There are other discouragements. We do not usually know

when we will be called during the debate. Thus the prospect is one of a long wait with no divertion save the contributions of friend and foe. Not everyone is worth listening to, and those that are good value frequently pinch the best bits of one's own speech. To those of a nervous disposition the strain of waiting can be very great, and the relief after speaking is overwhelming. No wonder so many of us suffer from IBS – the irritable bowel syndrome. The custom of the House calls for a speaker who has just sat down to show the good manners that are required to sit through the speech of the MP called immediately after him – a courtesy which can be hard to sustain.

The best time for a backbencher to speak is immediately after the front bench, ministers having usually gabbled through a civil servant's brief, pausing only to scratch their private parts. If he is an infrequent performer, as I have become, he can generally rely on being called quickly. If he is invariably brief and to the point, as I can be, he is even more likely to be favoured by the chair. Speakers and their deputies are human too. They are as stuffed full of oratory as a Strasbourg goose of grain. Ministers read their speeches, and so do members of the Opposition front bench. As they can place their texts on the dispatch boxes, they can read in comfort. The backbencher, on the other hand, hovers precariously over the bench in front, his seat catching him behind his knees, his notes clutched in his right hand. If he attempts to read, the House will resound with cries of 'reading', a facility which convention denies to backbenchers. It is better to have been properly rehearsed, or, if not, to rely only on note headings. To make a good speech in the House is a heady pleasure; to make a bad one is to feel like a music-hall performer who has been given the bird. Perhaps the most disconcerting thing of all is to realise quite suddenly that nobody is actually listening to what you are saying.

Having spoken it is important to go upstairs after an hour or so has elapsed, to the room where the *Hansard* writers prepare their copy. As the evening progresses the room is full of MPs correcting their copy. I try to turn mine into prose. Enoch Powell was the only MP I can remember who actually spoke in paragraphs; the syntax displayed by the rest of us stands in urgent need of re-decoration. The speech in the House can attract attention. It could be reported briefly in the quality dailies, or be featured in the parliamentary 'scene' which has become the favoured way of political reporting. Simon Heffer of the *Daily Telegraph*, Matthew Parris of *The Times*, Mark Lawson of the *Independent* and Andrew Rawnsley of the *Guardian* are members of the Taper School of Journalism. Bernard Levin, in the days before he took to his heels across Europe for the cameras, was the author of the 'Taper' column in Brian Inglis's *Spectator*. Levin treated the House as if it were a theatre, and his disrespectful style has, thirty years later, become the norm. We are now the Theatre of the Relatively Absurd. Were I to abandon politics and be obliged to get a proper job in order to sustain a pack of ungrateful dependants, I might try my hand, but I doubt whether I could sustain so frequent an attendance.

The days have gone, I am sorry to say, when *The Times* published its splendid parliamentary page that began with the unchanging formula: 'The Lord Chancellor took his seat on the Woolsack at half past two o'clock.' It is today quite an achievement for a member of either House to have his speech reported. In the old days *The Times* even awarded consolation prizes. The report always ended with a full list of the names of Members who had spoken but were not worth quoting. It was like one of those 'progressive' schools where the staff tell worrying parents that although we cannot all be high fliers, they believe in rewarding effort.

The posher papers still go through the motions of providing a parliamentary service. But a careful look will show that, the 'scene' apart, and not always then, relatively little that is printed deals with the debates. Most of it is about what happened at Question Time. Part of the explanation is, I believe, technical. In the old days, up to three or four years ago, when the newspapers were still living in the days of Caxton, it was possible for us to have a report of what our colleagues said at 10 o'clock the previous evening on our breakfast table. Now that the unions have been brought to Wapping and technology has been computerised, it takes longer to get the news into print. A morning paper can just about cope with Question Time. But only the most important news merits holding the presses. So if Kenneth Baker, for example, merely delivers something like the Gettysburg Address when winding up the evening's debate, there will not be a line of it in the papers next morning; whereas if a minister's teenage daughter is unlucky enough to be found at midnight *in flagrante delicto* in a squat in Catford, the *Sun* will clear its front page.

Most MPs have come to accept that so far as much of the media are concerned, we exist to entertain rather than to inform, or educate. One of the saddest sights in the tea room at Westminster is that of a high-minded young Conservative MP fighting back the tears as he leafs through the papers and finds not a single line about his carefully balanced case, representing as it did long hours reading Central Office's *Notes on Current Politics*. But newly elected Tory MPs are impossible to deflate. Within ten minutes he will be consoling himself with the thought that his views on the harmonisation of goat cheese tariffs throughout the Community will be picked up in Friday's *Economist* or win a mention on Radio 4's 'The Week in Westminster'.

But if the news we would all like to see is no longer there, the numbers of journalists accredited to the Palace of Westminster shows no sign of decreasing. The Members' Lobby is filled with them, importuning the newsworthy, gossiping with the unreliable and sucking desperately on the ends of their pencils. We have been sharing our premises with them, more or less amicably, for the best part of a century. It is rather like doctors seeing to it that offices should be provided within their hospitals for undertakers. In 1959, when one could tell a Tory from a socialist by looking at his boots, the journalists did better than we did for accommodation. We were given a locker big enough for a box of 12-bore cartridges, several back numbers of *Country Life* and a pair of waders. An accredited journalist was entitled to a desk. We were not. But we have done better in recent years.

If you stand in Parliament Square of an evening, when the lights of Whitehall have long been extinguished, look at the Gothic wing of the Palace that stretches along to Big Ben. The windows will still be lit. That is the corridor where the press have their offices. Somewhere up there in no man's land, they have their own restaurant and bar, out of the profits of which the books of our own Refreshment Department are properly balanced.

The parliamentary press corps are as mixed a bunch as Mrs

Thatcher's New Conservative party. There are the solemn short-hand writers whose frightening speed (they work for twenty minutes at a time) provides the basic reports on which the news agencies rely. There are the solid citizens who are the representatives of the provincial press, men who wear waistcoats, in whom some of the old-fashioned virtues of journalism still survive. Many of them have, over the years, forged close links with their local MPs, and indeed some, such as Joe Haines who now does for Robert Maxwell what he did so long and successfully for Harold Wilson, have become figures in their own right. And there are the television journalists, trim figures in bespoke suits, who deliver their reports to camera in incomprehensible accents, standing either on College Green with the Lords behind them, or posed prettily in front of Big Ben. The sketch-writers make up the highest caste of all, although their parliamentary victims may consider them to be as untouchable as they are unspeakable.

I have already listed the present practitioners of their art. There have been some memorably funny sketches. At his best, Frank Johnson when he was writing for the *Daily Telegraph* and then for *The Times* was an outstanding comic writer by any standards. Sadly, he left in order to play Hamlet. But the best examples of the sketch-writer's art are more than just funny. A good theatre or television critic is a pleasure to read, but also by probing to discover what it is the playwright is up to, he can substantially increase our understanding of life. By the same token an intelligently written 'sketch' can explain the workings of politics and politicians more effectively than any number of textbooks.

Norman Shrapnel of the *Guardian* was a great sketch-writer. He was essentially a man of letters, untrained in the political black arts, who treated his seat in the press gallery as if it were the dress circle. Apart from writing like an angel, he was eminently qualified to judge which of the men and women he was observing were on the way up, or down, and which of them were pompous humbugs. The sketch-writers are complemented by the lobby correspondents whose brief it is to report less on what happens in the Commons Chamber than on what is going on behind the scenes.

The lobby men are the pencil-suckers I referred to earlier. The lobby system seems to have come into being in the Phineas Finn days of Victorian Parliaments when the precincts of the Palace of Westminster were thronged by layabouts, most of whom were cadging some sort of commercial benefit for themselves, but some of whom were looking for scraps of scandal for one or other of the gossip sheets of the time. Today's tabloids are as British as the football hooligan, and both can trace their ancestry back for two hundred years. The Serjeant-at-Arms arranged to bring order into the system by drawing up a list of respectable newspapers who would have a right to a representative with access to the Members' Lobby, so that they could legitimately buttonhole Members, including ministers, and talk to them informally. With this privilege of access went rules.

The activities of the lobby have been expanded, but the basic rule under which members of it are licensed to operate is unchanged: if they talk to an MP, within or beyond the Commons, on 'lobby terms', they are free to make use of the information provided, but not to identify him or quote what he has said directly. The less experienced MP who has been telephoned at home by a 'reporter' say, of the *Daily Mail*, can find himself in trouble. Every word he says to the reporter is regarded by the reporter as fair game for he is not the *Mail*'s political and lobby correspondent. It is for the MP to beware. Under such circumstances he cannot expect to go 'off the record'. If an MP decides to use the press to further some campaign, as I did at the time of the launch of Conservative Centre Forward, secrecy may well be advisable. If the *Guardian* comes out with a story to the effect that 'left-wing Tory backbenchers fear the Government is planning to impose a special poll tax on mentally handicapped unmarried mothers', and if a Tory whip just happened to have seen a certain 'moderate' Conservative setting off the previous day in a taxi with the *Guardian*'s lobby man for lunch at the Neal Street Restaurant (very good Italian food but very noisy), he may just be smart enough to put two and two together.

There was once a Labour MP, long since gone, who never seemed to make a speech or ask a question, and never had any prospects of getting into Government, but who went round the House a happy man, obviously confident that he was an individual to be sought out. He was. He had a remarkable talent much appreciated by the lobby. He possessed a photographic memory. Without having taken notes, he could emerge from the weekly meeting of the parliamentary Labour party and offer a blow-by-blow account, an account that was winging its way to the newspapers within the hour. If a Tory leaves a meeting of the '22 (the committee comprising all Tory MPS who are not ministers) while it is still in progress, he will be followed down the committee corridor by the importunate scribbler. At such meetings it is customary for the chairman to call for secrecy, but without success. The chairman and the executive of the '22 now make it their business to issue a statement to the press themselves after every meeting, thereby at least getting their version of events into print. Outside the Whips' Offices there are no secrets at Westminster.

The lobby system is presently under attack. The *Independent* newspaper, for example, does not make use of it. The complaints arise from the way in which governments have found it convenient to use the lobby as an extension of their own public relations. Mrs Thatcher has used her press secretary, Bernard Ingham, shamelessly to rubbish those members of her cabinet who disagree with her. It was at such a meeting that John Biffen, while still a member of her cabinet, was described as 'a semi-detached member of the cabinet'. Backbenchers do complain that ministers find it all too convenient to make use of the lobby to announce plans when they ought to make an announcement to the House.

The advantage to the Government is obvious. It can fly kites. Take the case of the Chancellor contemplating whether to do away with mortgage tax relief. If he makes a speech suggesting the desirability of such a thing, he runs the risk of stirring up a hornets' nest. He may then have to back down, and suffer from what is now called 'a loss of credibility'. But if he merely drops a hint, off the record, over lunch with Simon Heffer of the *Daily Telegraph* at the Grill Room at the Dorchester, he can sit back and watch the reaction to Heffer's story. The idea may catch fire. Editorials in its favour may appear elsewhere. If not, then all the Chancellor has to do is to deny that he has any such proposal in mind. 'I never pay any attention to press speculation.' The *Daily Telegraph* has no comeback; the conversation, having been on lobby terms, never took place.

The conversation in question, according to the mystique of the lobby, never took place even when it was held in a large room full of people, which is how a large part of the off-the-record briefings have been taking place for years. When MPs first became aware of this after the war, they were so upset that they organised a rota (kept by Sir Herbert Williams) for keeping watch in the corridor leading to the room in a remote corner of the Palace where these meetings 'did not' take place. The idea was that if the MP on watch spotted a meeting in progress he spread the word so that his colleagues could judge for themselves what credence to give stories appearing in next morning's papers.

The lobby can visit No. 10 and No. 11. They go to the Prime Minister, Mrs Thatcher does not go to them. There are legitimate forms of kite-flying and more distasteful forms. Government PR started under Ramsay MacDonald who added a Private Secretary (Intelligence) to the No. 10 staff, called George Steward. It is from such small beginnings that the monster of modern governmental PR has grown. Every department now has a team of information officers, who, when they are not tipping off the press anonymously, take their orders from their minister. Their activities are co-ordinated by Steward's successor, Bernard Ingham. Ingham is now called the Prime Minister's press secretary, possibly because the word 'intelligence' has sinister connotations.

It is the task of the lobby correspondent to sift the information which he constantly receives. Most are astute men who know when they are being taken for a ride. But they are in a quandary. Just as the information officers are obliged to pump out information and disinformation at the behest of their masters, so the editors and news editors press the lobby correspondent to produce copy. Newspapers appear seven days a week and, whether or not the 'news' is genuine, have to fill their pages.

My Conservative MP may spend the evening in the Chamber listening to the debate. On the other hand he may abandon oratory in favour of attendance upstairs at one of many party committees. The party committees were invented, according to Harold Macmillan, before the war in order to keep MPs out of mischief. There is a party committee for every topic. Elections for officers are held annually, an occasion when the two 'wings' of the Conservative Party compete against each other for the votes of backbenchers. The defence committee, for example, elects a chairman, three vice-chairmen and a secretary who constitute the core of the committee. Meetings are held every Thursday evening at 5 p.m. in Room 10, meetings which are advertised in the weekly Whip and are open to the party as a whole.

Such meetings are addressed by a variety of speakers over the year. The Secretary of State will attend. So too will his ministers. The Chief of Staff, the Chief Scientist at the Ministry of Defence, defence correspondents of the national press, and academics who specialise in security matters, all will be invited to attend. The officers of the committee decide who shall speak, and issue the invitations. A party whip is detailed to 'look after' the committee (each Tory whip will have several such committees to oversee), and it will be his task to report back to the Chief Whip if anything is said or done which may be of significance. There are over a dozen such committees: they become more important when the party is in opposition for the officers serve as *de facto* front-benchers, speaking on their special subjects. I did so in the late 'seventies in my capacity as chairman of the media committee and one of the vice-chairmen of the party's defence committee.

Most days party committees are run-of-the-mill events. They become important when circumstances make them so. For example, the Chancellor will go upstairs to talk to the party's finance committee as soon as he has finished his budget speech in the chamber. The most exciting committee meeting I ever attended was in 1982, when, after the Argentinians invaded the Falklands, the House sat for the first time on a Saturday. Lord Carrington, the Foreign Secretary, was summoned to address a meeting of the combined foreign and defence committees upstairs. Mrs Thatcher had made what was probably her lamest speech in the Chamber, and the party was reeling from shock and indignation. There was to be blood all over the floor. As he climbed on to the platform, Peter Carrington said to me, 'If the buggers want my resignation they can have it'. He resigned three days later.

The party committees, covering as they do every possible subject of interest, serve as an adult education course for Members of Parliament. The MP, thirsty for knowledge, and wishing to be reasonably well informed, could spend the hours between 4 and 6, four afternoons a week, moving gently from one meeting to another: listening to Sir William Clark on finance, Sir Geoffrey Johnson Smith on defence, and Jim Lester on matters of employment. Attendance is usually small; defence attracts a loyal handful of MPs and some ancient peers, but attendance can rise dramatically. The Carrington meeting to which I have just referred must have been attended by 250 Tory MPs. By 6 in the evening, MPs feel that they have done enough; they have an hour or so to prepare themselves for the ordeal by hospitality which is all too frequently our lot.

If the whip is not a 'running' one, that is if the votes are expected at fixed times, MPs can go home to dinner or even go out to dinner, always provided that they leave in time to be back to vote at 10. MPs are notoriously unsatisfactory dinner guests; we tend to monopolise the conversation, embarrass our hostesses by talking in familiar terms about 'Margaret' and 'Neil', and break up the party by leaving the table before the pudding. Peter Bottomley's strictures have cut down the amount of wine drunk, but the garrulous MP in a dinner jacket in the Aye Lobby at 10 o'clock is still a common sight. But, by then, we are all a bit flushed. If we are not dining out, we must dine in. Solitaries eat pie and salad in the tea room. The more cheerful dine in the Members' Dining Room where they go in search of congenial company. The less fortunate stand ready to dine 'downstairs'.

The terrace floor of the Palace contains several private dining rooms which are hired out to various organisations. No public dinner can be held without the sponsorship of an MP, which means, of course, that he is obliged to attend. He will act as host either to a Conservative constituency dinner, his own or someone else's, and MPs spend a good deal of time taking in each others' washing, or as host to some firm or trade association. This he may do as part of a consultancy arrangement whereby he is paid a fee for services rendered. The very rich and successful MP will accept the use of a motor-car and chauffeur in lieu of a taxable lump sum.

How best to cope with dinners of this sort? It can only be done with the help of alcohol. The specially printed menus (which can be the first to tell you that you are expected to 'say a few words' after the Queen), over-cooked veg followed by a dish of Cabinet Pudding, and we must not forget the House of Commons's Senegalese claret, can bring about a feeling of cafard. Such entertainment does not constitute an ideal end to a difficult day. Nevertheless, as the level of conversation rises with the temperature, the effect of alcohol takes over, numbing a sense of discomfort, the effort of straining to catch the mumbled observations of a neighbour, and the pain caused by the sharp edge of a large plate of over-done lamb thrust unwittingly into the back of one's head by a harrassed waitress. In response to a comment, I agree cheerfully enough that Westminster is indeed the Mother of Parliaments. It is in this way that we get through the earlier part of the night. At 10 o'clock the division bells will ring, and as an added precaution, the door will be thrown open and a policeman's head will yell 'dee-vision'. Released, like so many greyhounds from a White City trap, a squad of MPs hurries to the lifts, making for the division lobby to cast their votes. Thank God, that at least is over.

The vote at 10 is always a parliamentary occasion. The sight, sound and smell of 372 Tory MPs crushed into a lobby the size of the Black Hole of Calcutta, waiting desperately for the doors to be opened by a flunky, will remain with me to my dying day. That and the sound of division bells. At 10, dinner has done its best or worst, and 'colleagues' who would not have exchanged a word at 7 now chat amicably enough to each other. A whip stands by the twin desks at which sit the clerks whose task it is to tick off our names as we pass by. His shouted message is that there will be 'another vote immediately'. As each vote takes twenty minutes (MPs have neither desks nor buttons, which in a sensible world would relieve us of this tiresome chore), the time of our departure for bed is delayed still further. When the Government's majority is 100, few bother to return to the Chamber to learn the result; we hang about in the Members' Lobby chatting to our friends until the bells ring for a second time.

By 10.30 I have had enough. This could be due to advancing years or to a lack of ambition. Nor do I share the zeal for Mrs Thatcher's counter-revolution which fires the enthusiasm and taps the stamina of true believers. I would not have made a good Cromwellian. If I disagree with a major piece of legislation such as the introduction of the poll tax, I say so, and stay away, but there is much besides about which I am, at best, equivocal. In the 'seventies I was an assiduous backbencher. I admired Ted Heath and approved of much that he was trying to do, particularly our entry into the European Community. I was cheerful enough the night we voted continuously through the night, from 10 p.m. to 10 a.m., going through the lobbies at twenty-minute intervals for the best part of twelve hours in favour of the reform of the trade unions. But I was fitter then.

If the business of the House continues after the two votes at 10, there is a scramble to find a pair, and then to register him with the staff of the Whips' Office. It could well be that the Opposition will not vote, not wishing to keep its own side out of the marital bed, but their intentions they will keep to themselves. Old friends on the other side will tip their pals the wink but fierce left-wingers are likely to keep silent. They tend to relish fighting the class war late at night. The trick under these circumstances is to watch the exits. If Labour MPs are seen heading for the cloakroom, they are more than likely to be followed, after a decent interval, by Tories.

In the old days the Tory whips used to man the exits, ready to cut off the line of retreat of their weaker brethren. A story of Sir Walter Bromley-Davenport's stint at the Whips' Office has passed into legend. The bluff Sir Walter, a former amateur heavyweight boxer, had only recently been made a whip. He spotted the retreating figure of a colleague whom he admonished. His victim took no notice and continued to make his escape. The enraged Sir Walter then booted him up the arse. The arse belonged to the Belgian ambassador. The postscript to this affair was even more significant: the gallant colonel was retired, only to be replaced by the young Edward Heath.

Backbenchers with nothing to lose can push off, at the cost of their reputation for loyal assiduity among the party whips. Ministers, on the other hand, unless they can get paired, or be given a bisque, which permits an infrequent absence, can find themselves patrolling the lobbies into the small hours after a hard day's work at the Ministry. And they will be expected to be at their desks at 9 o'clock the next day. I am very glad I am not a minister.

# 5

# *Snakes and Ladders*

IT IS the ambition of the newly elected MP of whatever party to become a minister, however junior. It was not always so. Even in 1959, when I was first elected to the Commons, there were in the Tory party grave men who made up the ballast of the party. If they had ever harboured ambition, it was long forgotten. To become 'the Member' was to extend or to fulfil their sense of social obligation. Engaged in country pursuits or in the casual exercise of city directorships, the 'Sir Hugh Monroe Lucas-Tooths' of their day were reluctant ministers.

Today, Mrs Thatcher has enfranchised the working class, and recast the Conservative party in its image. With few exceptions Tory MPs seek election to Parliament in order to attain ministerial office. Thirty years ago I certainly hoped to do so. There is no need to apologise: 'fame is the spur'. But how best to achieve office? How to win a transfer from the massed ranks of the unregarded? For twenty-five years I have been witness to the promotion of friend and foe, the soles of whose feet I have observed on the rungs of the ladder of success. How on earth did they do it?

The obvious answer is 'on their merits' but the process is sufficiently arcane to deserve closer scrutiny. It should first be pointed out that there can only be a hundred or so ministers at any one time; the Tory party in the House today has 372 MPs. The odds therefore of attaining ministerial office are three to one against. Many will call but few are answered. The Tory party's Whips' Office acts as talent scout, and it is the Chief Whip, acting perhaps on the recommendation of other members of his office, who is responsible for nine promotions out of ten. The tenth is appointed by Mrs Thatcher herself. Mrs Edwina Currie was sent to the Department of Health and Social Security over the objections of the Whips' Office and the same may have been true of the elevation in July 1988 of Eric Forth, an unattractively dogmatic right-wing Scotsman who sits for a Worcestershire seat. He went to the Department of Trade and Industry as dogsbody. His backbench colleague, Robert Rhodes James, complained publicly about his promotion, the first time in my experience that any MP had done so about another's elevation.

What is it the whips are looking for? It could be 'bottom', whatever that might mean. It will certainly be loyalty, the cement that keeps a broad church together. It could be ability, although intelligence is not enough on its own. It might even be expertise. But what are civil servants for? What I think they are looking for, above anything else, is predictability. The party whips do like to know where they stand. The whips are, of course, fellow Conservative MPs whose task it is to see to it that the Government gets its legislation through the House. They are as loyal as hound-dogs and pass, in their own right, for members of the Government. In the past the Tory Whips' Office was the haunt of adjutants drawn from the Household Division who were themselves largely without ambition (Ted Heath was the exception to the rule). Today, the office is run by ex-ministers (David Waddington, a recent 'chief', was at the Home Office), and staffed by a *corps d'élite* of younger Tories who use time spent in the Whips' Office as a springboard to greater things. 'Only the best' has become the motto of the office: those of us languishing on the backbenches who would gain ministerial 'life', must first lose it.

The whips are silent: they do not speak in the House or at the '22. They are the eyes and ears of the Government. Each is made responsible for a batch of backbenchers. These so-called 'area whips' keep in touch. If an MP fails to vote, his area whip will want to know the reason why. If an MP has doubts about some aspect of the Government's intentions or policies, he will be expected to tell his whip who, in his turn, should be quick to spot dissent and to head it off, either by explanation, cajolery or threats. The area whip is armed with the telephone numbers and addresses of his flock. These will include his matrimonial home, his London 'pad' and any other address of the sort that gave Oscar Wilde's tradesmen so much confidence. Tucked away in the suite of rooms which make up the 'office', situated next to the Members' Lobby, are the records: files in which the attitudes, sins, strengths and, most particularly, the weaknesses of Members of Parliament are carefully noted down.

When the House is sitting there is always a whip 'on the bench'. He is to be found on the front bench almost at the feet of the Speaker. He will attend Question Time. He will take a watch during debates, holding in his hand a clip-board on which he jots down remarks on a Tory member's contribution. Other MPS sitting directly behind him will strain to read his judgements which often turn out to be banal in the extreme. 'Unsound', or 'the usual nonsense', or 'attacked the Government'; sometimes a supportive speech is strongly recommended. Later, like a satiated bee, he will return to the hive laden with information. He is on the look-out for good speeches, that is ones in which loyalty and fluency happily co-exist. After a bill receives its second reading, as we have seen, it is taken 'upstairs' for its committee stage, where a team of members largely chosen by the Whips' Office scrutinises the legislation line by line in order to return it to the floor of the House for report and a third reading. The committee stages of bills are often as dull as dogs, but they do provide a chance for the ambitious to shine. 'He's bloody good on committee' is high praise when it comes from a member of the Whips' Office. What I think is meant is that the MP concerned was both articulate and supportive and capable of being both well into the watches of the night.

It might be fun to examine the careers of those of us who first entered the Commons in 1959. James Prior was made PPS, that is Parliamentary Private Secretary to Ted Heath. He had a First in estate management. He was also a Tory moderate at a time when moderates ruled, OK? He did not suffer from the ideological exclusion which was the fate of the young John Biffen (elected in '61) under the pre-Thatcher leadership. Nicholas Ridley, a second son who studied engineering, achieved junior office in the early 'seventies, but fell foul of the party leadership. He later became a gentleman monetarist, possibly the only one, and rose steadily under the patronage of Mrs Thatcher. As Secretary of State for the Environment he was probably the most politically unpopular member of the third Thatcher administration.

William Compton Carr went to prison. Philip Hocking did not return after his defeat in the 1964 election. Sir William Clark, a nice old thing, known to the irreverent as 'the Rotarian-General', never left the backbenches. Christopher Chataway, who in the early 'sixties was the party's 'golden boy', achieved junior office under Harold Macmillan and more senior office under Ted, but retired from Parliament in the mid-seventies to pursue a career in banking. Had he stayed put he would have been a member of the first of Mrs Thatcher's cabinets though probably not of the later ones. He was ideologically 'unsound'; a Tory of moderate persuasion having little in common with shopkeepers. Promotion does depend upon the current fashion in ideology.

Sir Peter Emery shone for a time under Ted Heath but was never in receipt of Mrs Thatcher's favours. Charles Longbottom left in '64 in order to get married. Mrs Thatcher was one of the first to win promotion; she did so under Harold Macmillan or, to be more precise, under Martin Redmayne who was Harold's Chief Whip. I have never received office. I was asked to become PPS to Mr Bernard Braine, at the time a junior minister at Health, but I was told by Michael Hughes-Young, the then Deputy Chief Whip, that 'the party would not wear it'. I have always been a little suspect. David Walder, a close friend who was in the Whips' Office during Ted Heath's premiership, told me that Francis Pym, at that time the Chief Whip, did not consider me to be a Conservative. I have long meant to ask him precisely what he thought I was. I was 'Conservative' enough to act as his *chef du cabinet* at the time of Conservative Centre Forward, Pym's abortive revolt in 1985. If under Ted Heath I was 'not one of us', the same could be said in spades for Mrs Thatcher's time in office.

There are several rungs to a candidate-minister's ladder. He can become a parliamentary private secretary to a minister. This task is rarely onerous, and can give a useful insight into the mind of a minister and the workings of his office. The PPS should become a dab hand with the tonic, a remover of overcoats, and a shoulder on which to cry. Much will depend upon the patron. Sir Geoffrey Howe invited Mrs Virginia Bottomley to be his PPS in 1987; the next year she was given junior ministerial office at the Department of the Environment.

Mrs Thatcher's PPS while in opposition was Fergus Montgomery. He did not win promotion but he did receive a knighthood. In Government, Mrs Thatcher first made the late Ian Gow, MP for Eastbourne, her PPS. Gow was given junior office in Northern Ireland, but, having fallen out of favour due to his opposition to the Anglo-Irish agreement, effectively exhausted his chances. Gow was succeeded by Michael Alison, a junior minister under Ted Heath. Alison, who has long been known as St Michael Alison, owing to his strongly held Christian beliefs, was never brought back into Government. He had to be content with a knighthood. St Michael was succeeded by Archie Hamilton, the largest Tory of them all, who, after his bag-carrying, was sent to the Ministry of Defence as a junior minister. The present incumbent is Mark Lennox-Boyd who can in turn look forward to his just desserts, driven, no doubt, into the obscurity of junior office by an Austin Princess.

The number of PPS's has grown markedly in recent years. Traditionally there were only three, one each for the Prime Minister, the Foreign Secretary and the Chancellor. Today every ministerial pipsqueak is encouraged to find a 'fag' of his own. This development is a whips' trick. The PPS is not a member of the Government, but he has been put on the 'pay-roll vote'; that is, were he to vote against the Government he would lose his post, and with it the chance of promotion to office proper. In this way the whips can tie up a large number of backbench MPs who might otherwise be free to roam the pastures of the Government's legislation, grazing where they might. To be a PPS is to place one's foot upon the lowest rung of the ladder of promotion but it would be unwise to put too much weight upon it.

Some Tory MPs move directly into the Whips' Office. Usually this is regarded as a signal mark of approval. But not all the members of the Whips' Office are high fliers. The office is not simply recruited on merit. Geography plays a part; so, too, does one's place in the political spectrum. The right as well as the left of the party must be represented. And there will always be room for the more pedestrian, the MP who is content to remain in the Whips' Office almost indefinitely, holding some archaic portfolio like the 'Master of the Queen's Horse', and making it his business to turn out the lights once the proceedings of the House of

Commons have come to an end. Under Martin Redmayne most whips were 'adjutants', today most of them are birds of passage, waiting to be wafted into the Department of Social Security with their own motor-car and civil service driver.

I would have enjoyed a period spent in the Whips' Office. It would have been fun to have been privy to so many secrets. The life of a secret policeman is not one long ball, but at least I would have been engaged, as a whip, in the practice of politics, in the taking of temperatures, in massaging the monstrous egos of one's colleagues or in twisting their puny arms. The secret of life at Westminster is to be busy rather than bored, and neglect, which is the sanction of the Whips' Office, leads ineluctably to mischief or boredom. Their carrots are promotion; their sticks, neglect. The Tory whips, known to the irreverent as the 'broederbund', are, in fact, a band of brothers who exclude by blackball those whose names might tentatively be suggested by their colleagues as possible members of their order. The flavour of the office is still faintly aristocratic, and their loyalty is to the party as well as to its leader. Tristan Garel-Jones has become, over the years, the archetypal Tory whip. Rich but not grand, moderate of view (he was an original member of the 'Blue Chips', a dining club of the most promising of the non-Thatcherite Tories of the 1979 intake), and possessed of fluent Spanish, Garel-Jones has moved steadily upwards through the hierarchy of the Whips' Office. At the time of writing he is the No. 2, having, while one rung below, been responsible for writing each parliamentary day a 750-word epistle to be sent by special post office messenger to Buckingham Palace for the Sovereign to read while she dresses for dinner. The senior whips are all Lords Commissioners, officers of the Household (Elizabeth's, that is, not Margaret's), sinecures which entitle two of them to ride in a coach in the procession to Parliament for the State Opening or to receive a haunch of venison culled from Richmond Park four times a year. (That privilege extends to all Ministers of State.) Garel-Jones does not ride in state; he remains behind in a room at the Palace furnished with sherry and a television set, as 'hostage' for the safe return of the Queen from Westminster.

The secrecy which surrounds the Whips' Office has always attracted the attention of the press. The office is the only body

within Parliament to which the lobby and the political correspondent have not got access. This can give rise to exaggeration: the
whips are frequently portrayed in newspapers as wielding more
power than they actually possess. The Government whips are
obliged to tread carefully. An MP threatened in some way by an
over-zealous whip can complain publicly to the Speaker and seek
his protection, the political parties having in fact no place in the
constitution. Any untoward pressure brought upon a Member of
Parliament either to vote or not to vote would be a breach of
Parliamentary privilege and punishable as such. The weekly
Whip is, despite the blackness of its ink, no more than a summons
to attend.

The confidentiality of the Whips' Office works to the advantage
of Members of Parliament. MPS can and do take their personal
crises, whether medical, financial or matrimonial, to the Whips'
Office, and are certain of finding a sympathetic ear. Debts have in
the past been paid off (although we should not take so happy a
service for granted), leave of absence given in the case of an
unhappy medical prognosis, and a discreet silence kept over
marital disagreements. By the same token the Whips' Office is
grateful for warning in advance of any scandal, particularly if it is
a matter of security. The lessons of the Profumo affair when an
unworldly Prime Minister, unworldly at least in sexual matters,
was deceived by his Minister of War, have been taken to heart.
The failings of 1963 were those of the Government Whips' Office.
Mr Martin Redmayne was as much an innocent as the Prime
Minister whose interests he was there to serve. 'Jolly Jack
Profumo' did enjoy a reputation of sorts, but one of which the
Whips' Office was not properly aware.

The Government Whips' Office is not regarded by other Tory
MPS as being unduly oppressive. Tory whips usually retain the
courtesies of the pre-Thatcher Conservative party. There have
been exceptions, for example, David Lightbown's rebuke of the
hapless Jerry Hayes who had the temerity to read out in
committee the past pronouncements of Our Great Leader on the
subject of charges for eyes and teeth. Mr Lightbown, whom many
Tories have in the past mistaken for an off-duty policeman,
clearly overstepped the mark. But he has a heart of gold. The
whips take care when dealing with their colleagues. Unlike the

Labour party, whose Whips' Office has something of the flavour of a Sergeants' Mess, and the bad language which goes with it, the Conservative party behaves with a certain decorum. Even today, it has the air of an Officers' Mess. I have overheard a Labour whip rebuking a Labour MP for some dereliction of duty in terms which, if used by one Tory to another, would be regarded as an outrageous breach of good manners. The Conservative party may have its complement of shits but they do not expect to be so described in public.

The Tory whips are great eaters. They are sent out daily either to lunch or to dine in the Palace of Westminster. Long hours and late nights suggest the need for refreshment, but their presence scattered throughout the Members' Dining Room is necessary for the collection of tidbits of information. Dressed in plain clothes and passing themselves off as 'one of the lads', the Tory whips can be the life and soul of a party of four. Tristan Garel-Jones told me that he got wind of the formation of Conservative Centre Forward in 1985 (Pym's Private Army) after Sir Ian Gilmour asked him his opinion of an obscure Tory backbencher. Such straws in the wind are gratefully gathered in. Why should Gilmour have been interested? The whips are determined that no meeting of Tory MPs, however small, or seemingly insignificant, should take place without their knowledge. MPs are inveterate gossips. Encouraged by the house claret, we have been known to tell all. Yet we are probably at our most vulnerable at tea-time. MPs flock into the tea room after Question Time or a Statement looking for the cup that cheers. Once again we are joined by members of the Whips' Office who, hiding behind their evening newspapers, do not miss a thing: opinion as to the quality of a minister's performance; the wisdom of the government's intentions; the foolishness of colleagues; or the wit and wisdom of the Prime Minister.

The Conservative Whips' Office remains the last bastion of male supremacy in the Palace of Westminster. At a time when the Tory party has been run by one woman for fifteen years, there has never been a woman in the Whips' Office. Why should this be? It could be that women are not clubbable, possessing a feline independence as opposed to a doggy conviviality. It could be that the rebuke to a male colleague, however understated, might not be as acceptable when delivered by a woman. Wives could object to a woman telephoning husbands at all hours, seeking their whereabouts. They might even bring their knitting into the whips' common room. I think this last is the real reason for their exclusion. The common room, around which the whips have their desks, is a masculine Eden into which even the most determined female Member of Parliament (to say nothing of snakes) will enter at her peril. Tory whips may take care not to swear at their flock but their language in private can be colourful. And has not the Conservative party done more than enough for women as it is?

The news of promotion to the front bench, when it comes, does so, not from the Prime Minister, but from the Chief Whip. In the aftermath of a general election, the aspirant will wait anxiously beside his telephone for the call. If it rings, then joy will be unconfined. One could, of course, be sent as parliamentary secretary ('parly-sec') to an unfashionable ministry such as Social Services or the Department of Trade and Industry. Welsh backbenchers are more than likely to be sent to the Welsh Office, Scots to brave the wrath of their fellow-countrymen. But for some there is the prestige of becoming a minister of the crown, the opportunity to be of service, and the chance of further promotion. However, the surge of adrenalin must be carefully distributed. For the pleasures of office may pale when the long hours, the tedious and repetitive work, which in many cases consists of signing, and thereby taking responsibility for, answers to the aggrieved constituents of other MPs, and the relative exclusion from the excitements of the Commons, are finally taken on board.

The parly-sec at the Department of Social Services is likely to serve in that office for two years. During that time he will perform in company with a minister of state and the Secretary of State twice a month at Question Time. Unless his subject comes suddenly into prominence, there will be no opportunity to shine in debate. He may, on the other hand, be given part responsibility for a contentious bill, an undertaking that will task his mastery over detail and his physical stamina. He will perform upstairs before a small committee of thirty-two MPs, drawn proportionately from the political parties. There will be no press or public.

Behind him will sit the whip, whose good opinion as to his performance can make or mar his prospects for promotion. He will occasionally lunch or dine in the Members' Dining Room, but he will suffer from a feeling of isolation both from people and events. Backbenchers can meet weekly at the '22, ridiculous though the proceedings often are: there is no such forum for junior ministers. It is not surprising that under such circumstances the opportunity to inspect the offices of 'the social' in some Northern city becomes a welcome opportunity to quit the office with its turgid routine. And in recess, when backbenchers enjoy a period of holiday which is longer than school holidays but not as extensive as university vacations, the minister is permitted his three weeks with bucket and spades. I hope I am not painting too gloomy a picture.

As the MP climbs the ladder from parly-sec to minister of state, and, if he is very talented or fortunate, into the cabinet, so the workload increases remorselessly. Civil servants delight in filling his red box with a night's homework. Backbenchers may spend the hours between 10 p.m. and midnight carousing with their mates in the Smoking Room, but ministers sit hunched over their desks in their offices below the chamber, 'attending to paper'. A moment's indiscretion with a journalist, and a time-bomb is placed beneath his desk. Wives are neglected, children ignored and personal finances suffer from the poverty of reward. Only Prime Ministers with millionaire husbands can afford the luxury of a gesture to take a cut in salary. A stint as junior minister at Health or Social Services can be a two-year sentence to hard labour with no remission. An Edwina Currie can rise above the anonymity, and do so with some style. But at some cost. The more modestly inclined soldier on in the belief that virtue is its own reward.

In the game of snakes and ladders, the longest 'ladder' still remains the speech in the Chamber. A brave speech, witty, pithy and unkind to the other side is the quickest way to achieve a reputation and with it the attention of the whips. The most poisonous 'snake' is undoubtedly the media. Compared with the temptations offered by the twin vipers of press and television, alcohol and adultery are grass snakes, benign, somnolent and dry to the touch. The newly elected MP becomes impatient. He finds it hard to catch the Speaker's eye, and he suffers the torments of the damned as his rivals spring into prominence. He can turn to the press as a vehicle for his opinions, a vehicle, what is more, that pays for the privilege of his custom.

In the early 'sixties I made the classic error of preferring to write for Brian Inglis's *Spectator* rather than striving to make supportive speeches in the Chamber. I was inexperienced, nervous, and poor. It was much easier to accept Inglis's invitation to write his 'Westminster Commentary' than to work up a speech, sit through a debate, sweating at the palms, never to be called upon to speak. I was quite unaware of the effect my scribblings had upon 'the colleagues'. Even had my views been entirely unexceptional (in which case I would not have been asked to write), the very fact of a Tory MP putting pen to paper was deeply shocking. It was simply 'not done'. At that time I was an enthusiastic supporter of Harold Macmillan. I was in favour of 'the wind of change' and strongly in favour of Britain's entry into the Common Market. Despite the Prime Minister's warning 'not to be impatient with the majors', I was very impatient with the old buffers who, sitting on the Tory benches, disapproved of Macmillan and all his works. I believe the veto exercised by the Deputy Chief Whip on the invitation I had received from Bernard Braine to become his PPS was due to my journalism.

Later I found myself a political commentator, a spectator of events in Westminster, and as such a frequent critic of different aspects of party policy. Early in the Thatcher years I moved defiantly into opposition, using humour as a weapon against her self-righteousness. Had Edward Heath won in February '74 I might have been given office (he has never said as much) but by the time Mrs Thatcher came to power I was all too plainly 'not one of us'. I make these personal observations solely to point the moral. It is hard to ride two horses at the same time.

There is another temptation related to the one to which I succumbed: that is to use the press in order to attract attention to oneself, not by writing articles but by the dissemination of the press release. MPs do play the old game of column inches, sending two short paragraphs to the news editors of newspapers, or of television, setting up their stall in the market of the instant quote, living with suitcase ready packed to travel to Granadaland or to the BBC's Television Centre. 'Disgusted Ealing' (Harry Greenway) or Anthony Beaumont-Dark are two of the most assiduous practitioners of this black art. They set up their tents in the studios of the 'World at One' and are faintly surprised when no one takes them very seriously.

In my first incarnation as MP for Rochester and Chatham I scanned the newspapers for those lists of 'coming men and women', 'faces for the 'sixties' and so on, hoping to find my name among them. I once did, and on the cover of the *Economist*. Beyond Westminster no one takes the slightest notice of them; inside the hothouse, they are scrutinised with all the care given to the casualty lists of the Great War. The advent of television will change the way in which the newspapers treat Westminster. The tabloids will carry more background information about MPs, television itself will focus upon the better-looking, the noisy and the cards. That way lie even greater perils for young men in a hurry.

# 6

# A Bit on
# the Side

LIFE AT the Palace of Westminster has its consolations. A Labour MP who later joined the Social Democrats, and promptly lost his seat, once said publicly that 'being an MP is better than working', and we all knew what he meant. The hours are long, and it is up to the Member to fill them as he thinks fit. For those not on the ministerial treadmill, it is as well to keep occupied. This is a maxim which applies with some force to those of us who have been left stranded on the backbenches.

What are the consolations of never having achieved office? They are travel, consultancy and the remorseless hospitality offered by those with something to sell. We are never bribed – it would not be worth anyone's while – but we can be seduced by a prawn cocktail. An industry has grown up around Westminster and Whitehall, its purpose persuasion and its method, entertainment. It is also much in evidence around Brussels and Strasbourg. Their black tents can be glimpsed from the windows of my tiny attic office where I sit at one or other of my two desks (or doze after lunch in my easy chair), equipped with a free telephone to anywhere within the United Kingdom (free calls abroad only on strictly Parliamentary business), and unlimited quantities of rather grand stationery. I have put a Ralph Wood pottery bust of Minerva on the top of my glass-fronted bookcase, in the hope of acquiring her wisdom. The public and parliamentary relations industry is the preserve of ex-MPs and party agents, and staffed by many who have failed for one reason or another to be elected to the House. Were Mrs Currie to devote herself as a backbencher to such 'consultancy' she would make her fortune. There is nothing wrong with their activities; in a plural society politics has

71

become a conflict of interests, each in competition with another for the ear of minister or mandarin.

Travel is the sweetener of public life. In my twenty-three years as an MP, I have travelled the world on a free ticket. I have been a delegate to three international assemblies: the Council of Europe, the Western European Union and the North Atlantic Assembly. I have also made use of the weekly Whip, which besides stern injunctions to attend contains discreetly worded invitations on behalf of the Anglo-American Parliamentary Association, or some such body, to apply for a week's visit to Kenya or wherever. 'Spouses are not invited,' we may learn with relief. Or, if they are, 'only at the Member's own expense'. Come fly with me and at the taxpayers' expense.

The invitation to be a delegate to one or other of the international assemblies (assemblies are parliaments which have not been elected; their membership is nominated from national parliaments), comes from the party whips. It is their largest and sweetest carrot. Their stick is exclusion from office. Invitations to tread the light fantastic in congenial places abroad are sent either as a reward, or as exile. I received my invitation to join the Council of Europe and the Western European Union in 1972 from Sir John Stradling Thomas who was then the Deputy Chief Whip. He told me I would have the time of my life and enjoy a tax-free income. He was right.

In the great days of European unity in the years after the war, the British delegation of 36 MPs, drawn in proportion from the three political parties in the House, consisted of politicians of the first class. The Tories included Winston Churchill, Harold Macmillan and Duncan Sandys (who survived into my day). More recently, the delegation has acquired something of the flavour of *le deuxième cru* as enthusiasm for Europe has melted in the heat of disappointment and the cruder nationalism of Mrs Thatcher. Membership has become the reward of those discharged from middle-ranking office, and a silk-lined dustbin for others whose chances of promotion have disappeared. It is a consolation prize. The really keen stand for the European Parliament.

I suppose the easiest way to receive invitations to travel abroad is to suck up to foreign governments, especially those which are unpopular. Ron Brown went to Afghanistan. Tory backbenchers who sympathise with the whites in South Africa, and some who do not, can be certain of an invitation to go on a fact-finding visit to the Republic; by the same token Labour MPs who have been sympathetic in the past to the Soviet Union have travelled freely within Russia and the countries of the Warsaw Pact. Some have made comfortable livings out of East/West trade at a time when there was precious little of it. Another way is to join one of the many Anglo-foreign parliamentary associations which have kept pace with the ever-increasing number of newly-independent states. I did once join the Anglo-Mexican Society, at the prompting of its chairman Sir John Rodgers, in the hope of a week in Acapulco, but the best I could manage was lunch at the Embassy in London.

More flatteringly, an invitation can come out of the blue from a London embassy. In the early 'sixties when I was MP for Rochester and Chatham in my first incarnation, the Cultural Attaché at the United States Embassy offered me a Smith-Mundt scholarship whereby the promising young politician who had not visited America might do so at the expense of their taxpayers. Having assured myself that the water was safe to drink, I leapt at the invitation and for six weeks at the beginning of 1963 toured the United States living 'high off the hog' on the hospitality of the natives and visiting several defence installations including Cape Canaveral and the Strategic Air Command HQ at Omaha, Nebraska.

At the Manned Space Center at Houston, Texas, I was greeted by every one of the twelve astronauts in training. *En route* my eye had caught a notice on the board which proclaimed the visit of 'Lord Julian Critchley' at 9 a.m. This description, if carried in the evening edition of the *Houston Bugle*, would have made me a social success, but I feared it might later be picked up by a British tabloid and retailed to my disadvantage. I broke the news to the dozen best-integrated men in America, at which eleven of them sloped off leaving me with the astronaut on duty. I still have, however, the photograph of all thirteen of us; it hangs in my Commons' office. Only three of us did not make the moon.

For six weeks or so I swung across America from Washington to New Orleans *via* Charlottesville. A professor of the University of Virginia whom I had met over drinks courteously told a call-girl the name of my hotel in New Orleans. She rang me one evening to suggest dinner. Such was traditional Southern hospitality. I went down into the bayou country by boat, accepted the key to the city (I am also an Admiral of the Nebraska Navy) and took breakfast at Brennan's. Sadly, I have never been back.

I was 32 and full of vigour. Even so, six weeks on the stump, entertaining and being entertained, catching early morning planes and arriving in time for those long drawn out American cocktail parties where the liquor is hard, and dinner distant, practically wore me out. I would never embark on a US-wide lecture tour, however handsome the rewards. The Grand Canyon was all it is cracked up to be (although the demands of my schedule prevented me from going down to the bottom and back on a mule), Las Vegas was hideous, and California got better the further north one travelled. I received a *per diem* of so many dollars a day, most of which returned home with me, and a large selection of books, mainly on matters of nuclear strategy. I wrestled with Herman Kahn at thirty thousand feet over Chicago.

A year later I paid two visits to the Far East and one to Ethiopia. 1964 was the year of 'confrontation'; war with Indonesia over disputed territories in Borneo. The Ministry of Defence flew me to Singapore where I stayed with the Governor, and to Kuching where a foolhardy ADC took me sea bathing, only for me to emerge with my feet covered in the poisonous spines of some sea urchin. I spent a day in bed under a slowly turning wooden fan, waited on hand and foot by a solicitous general. Later the Ministry of Defence sent me to Woomera in the company of Alun Gywnne Jones of *The Times*, to see a Blue Steel missile being fired from a Vulcan bomber. The firing aborted at the count of two, and the somewhat embarrassed Australians took the party on a week-long tour of the Snowy Mountain Irrigation Scheme. We sat cheerfully in the back of a bus admiring the girls and eating Australian mutton for dinner. The Inter-Parliamentary Union footed the bill for my visit to Haile Selassie's Ethiopia. We dined in a setting worthy of Cecil B. de Mille. The election of October 1964 put an end to my junketting. I lost my seat to Mrs Anne Kerr by 2,000 votes. In five years in the House I had visited South Africa, courtesy of Granada Television after the Sharpeville massacre, the United States, Cyprus, Aden and South

74

Yemen, Borneo, and several continental European countries. Defeat at Chatham succeeded in clipping my wings.

What I have recounted was not serious travel. Pleasure took me round the world; duty to Strasbourg and the Council of Europe. Membership of the British delegation to the Council of Europe (*'cette assemblée moribonde au bord du Rhin'* was de Gaulle's view of it) meant some very serious junketting indeed. An international assembly or talking shop of the democratic states of Western Europe including and beyond the countries of the EEC, it was based in Strasbourg where it enjoyed the worst climate and the poorest communications of anywhere in France. But it did possess fine wines of a high acidic content and a cuisine which was robustly Franco-German.

The wines of the country are an easily-acquired taste. They are invariably white, and liverish even when not drunk to excess, and we soon became addicted to the gewurztraminer, the riesling, the tokay and the pinot gris. Elderly knights of the shires would keep a bottle of the late-gathered in the bidet, packed in ice, as a midnight comforter. The food was French, the portions, German. I imagine it was John Rodgers himself, the leader of our delegation, who took me on one side during my first visit to Strasbourg in '72 and told me of the advantages of political service abroad. 'The food, dear boy, is better, and the oratory largely incomprehensible.'

It was hard not to fall in love with Strasbourg. Its medieval centre was as black and white as a Herefordshire village but without the smells. The suburbs owed much of their style to Imperial Germany which occupied the city from 1870 until 1918 and then again during the Second World War. The old city was interlaced with canals on which the delegates would ride in boats during the long afternoons of early summer, chatting up the ladies of the Corps of Interpreters, a fine body of girls who travelled Europe in the wake of *les parlémentaires*. The Top Tories led by Sir John Rodgers, the MP for Sevenoaks, a nice old thing of a formidable conviviality, would stay at the Hôtel Sofitel; the leader in his suite, his acolytes in comfortable rooms furnished in something of the American style of *les grands hôtels internationaux*, large lamps and small fridges. I put up at the Hôtel Gutenberg, once the favourite hotel of the *Wehrmacht*, situated next to the one-spired cathedral with its bells and storks.

The Council of Europe had no power but it did have a high moral content. It met three times a year for a week or more, but its many committees travelled the world in an all year round attempt to derive sufficient information for the publication of a series of reports which were debated and voted on at the meetings of the assembly. It had its serious side. Sir Frederic Bennett, the MP for Torquay who succeeded Sir John as our great leader, was responsible for the entry of Liechtenstein into the comity of nations. In return, he and others were given funny medals by a funny grand duke. The council was staffed by an international bureaucracy and in receipt of its own ambassadors representing the member states. It struck, and indeed still does strike, attitudes on any of the political and social problems facing 'Europe'. When I first went to Strasbourg the Assembly was housed in a prefabricated building facing a park in the northern suburbs of the city. The park contained an undistinguished restaurant much in demand for *vins d'honneur*, and a zoo where the prettier young matrons would take their children on tours of inspection. The park itself was patrolled by uniformed attendants, small men in uniform, who would pursue those of us who walked across the grass blowing shrilly upon their whistles. It would be hard to say whether the zoo or the Assembly attracted the more visitors for Europeans take 'Europe' seriously, and the galleries were always full of parties of schoolchildren.

Service at Strasbourg was coupled with membership of the Western European Union the headquarters of which was in Paris. It was a tale of two cities. The WEU was the child of the Brussels Treaty of 1948, the seven signatories foreshadowing the Nato Treaty itself. The WEU was a defence assembly; it had no moral content. Its remit was to examine the military and political problems confronting the Western alliance and to write reports upon them, reports which would be debated at the Assembly which met twice a year, December and June, in Paris. The committees, like those of the Council of Europe, travelled the world in search of fact and opinion. I took the WEU seriously and became the chairman of its Defence and Armaments Committee, where, with the help of Stuart Whyte, a bearded English clerk, I

wrote more reports on defence problems than any of my predecessors.

The twice yearly meetings of the WEU were held in the Avenue
Wilson (Woodrow not Harold) in a nasty, brutish building put up
in the style of the Third Reich in the 8 ème arrondissement. The
form was much the same as at Strasbourg. A series of reports
would be debated by the Assembly and voted upon with the
French delegation invariably voting against. We would be paid
visits by the great. The Secretary of State for Defence would fly
out from London for the day and deliver a speech prepared for
him by his private office. The French Foreign Minister would
arrive and flirt outrageously with the Assembly, promising to
rescue it from the decent obscurity into which the Anglo-
Americans had deliberately let it fall. The attitude of France
towards Nato and collective Western defence was, in my time,
still flavoured by the hostility of de Gaulle's desire for French
independence; it is only in recent years that the French and their
Nato allies have grown closer together.

Who could complain of a fortnight's holiday a year spent in the
most beautiful city in the world and paid for by the taxpayer at
the rate of £70 a day? I had been a student at the Sorbonne in the
early 'fifties and to return to the haunts of my youth twenty-five
years on was pleasure indeed. Paris had changed a little. Gone were
the buses with open platforms at the back, the klaxons had been
silenced by Presidential decree and the shabby bars of the Left
Bank, all zinc and brown paint, had been smartened up beyond
recognition. When the debates in the Assembly were duller even
than usual I would take the Métro to the end of the line, sitting with
my copy of *France Soir* in a red first-class carriage recapturing my
lost youth. That unique smell of mingled sweat, garlic and cheap
scent never fails to do for me what the *madeleine* did for Proust, or
the wartime memory of Paris for Palinurus.

Politics abroad has a glamour to it which backbenchers at home
never enjoy. We were treated like ministers of the Crown.
Ambassadors would be placed at our disposal. We would be
invited to lunch or to dine at the British Embassy and the
Chambre des Députés. At one such Embassy lunch the topic of
the Windsors cropped up. It must have been at the time of the

Thames TV series on the life of Edward VIII. I asked how was Mrs Simpson. 'You mean the Duchess of Windsor,' corrected the Greek-born wife of Sir Nicholas Henderson, our ambassador. She then told of dining with the Windsors in Paris. The food was wonderful – the Windsors had the best chef in Paris, and after dinner the party moved into the drawing room where the Duke solemnly embroidered the legend 'I love you' on to a piece of cloth and presented it formally to the Duchess. 'Very un-British' was Lady Henderson's comment.

The reward for those of us who had written a report was a formal lunch at one of the great restaurants of Paris. I stayed either with friends in Neuilly or in cheap hotels in the Quartier Latin, although try as I might I could never book in to the hotel, let alone the room, in which Oscar Wilde died. It was invariably taken by Americans. Evenings would be spent in congenial company. We fell in and out of love. We worried about the state of the alliance, and of our digestions. Politically cossetted in way that we would not have been at home, we were living happily, well above our station.

To those MPS whose experience of Europe had previously been limited to a fortnight spent on the Costa Brava, service abroad was an education of sorts. The Council of Europe and the WEU were regarded by nearly everyone as a jolly, giving a chance to enjoy *'la politique des vacances'*, eight weeks a year away from wives, constituency agents and party activists. The official proceedings attracted little or no attention in the British press, and the reports, compiled so laboriously by the committed few, were rarely, if ever, debated on the floor of the House of Commons. My interest was in defence matters so I took the WEU more seriously than I did the Council of Europe.

Yet it was all a waste of time. I was in my forties; most of the other members of the delegation were much older. They had seen service at home and were enjoying a well-earned reward. Duncan Sandys, Sir Harwood Harrison and Lord St Helens; their names are a roll-call of a forgotten Tory party. I was, however, in exile. Labour MPS, on the other hand, served for a shorter time on the British delegation and were recruited from across the spectrum of the party's talent. We were the remittance men. I abandoned the Council of Europe and WEU in 1979, and having failed to get office in the first of Mrs Thatcher's administrations, accepted yet another whip's invitation to become a member of the party's delegation to the North Atlantic Assembly.

The Nato parliamentarians enjoyed an annual assembly (usually held in the cities of Southern Europe to be certain of attracting the Americans). We lived a full committee life. The addition of senators and congressmen gave us a better tone, and the quality of the national delegations was much higher. The form was much the same as before. Hospitality was spiced with debate and it involved a good deal of trans-Atlantic travel. The most popular junket of them all was the 'Nato Tour' which is organised each August. A military aircraft is placed at the disposal of those willing to attend and the world is their oyster. We flew in the last Britannia turbo-prop in the Royal Air Force. In 1979 I spent a fortnight flying around Europe from the submarine pens of La Rochelle to the Kurfürstendamm in Berlin, cossetted all the way. My most vivid memory is of being entertained by the Luftwaffe near Munich who flew us in and out of the Alps in their helicopters; a breathtakingly exciting afternoon of mountain flying and gentle aerobatics. Another Tory MP in the party had the curious habit of spending the night at each and every city we visited on the town with the local police vice squad. He would leave on arrival at the airport under escort only to rejoin the party the morning after for the next lap of the journey.

As a member of the Nato Assembly, and rapporteur of its Nuclear Weapons Committee (together with John Cartwright, later to become the SDP's chief whip) I visited Madeira, Venice, Washington and The Hague. The chairman of the committee was Senator Joe Biden, later to be accused of pinching Neil Kinnock's perorations.

But I was growing tired of airports: the interminable hassle of delayed flights, lost luggage and uncomfortable seats. After the 1983 election I called it a day. I had accumulated a library of reports on defence matters and made friends across the Alliance. I had developed a taste for Alsatian wines. I had seen the world but I would have done better, politically that is, to have stayed at home.

Travel is not the only perk that MPs enjoy. Consultancy is another. This is a development of the notion that MPs are invariably invited to become directors of public companies because 'it looks good to have a Member's name on the board'. In fact, few MPs today are given seats on boards of directors. If we are in demand it is to open the doors of Whitehall, and we are asked to do so in our capacity as 'consultants'. We can be approached either by lobbies such as the Gun Lobby, which had an interest in amending Home Office legislation to restrict the ownership of guns embarked on in the aftermath of the Hungerford Massacre of 1987, or by defence-manufacturing companies anxious to win contracts from the Ministry of Defence. Every trade association will have its 'parliamentary adviser' who enjoys a retainer of several thousand a year. Even the Police Federation employs an MP to act as its spokesman.

No harm is done, provided the MP in question fills in his 'interests' in the Parliamentary Register. Not much good is done either. The MP who speaks for the police carries no greater weight with his colleagues for doing so. In fact, he probably carries less. Consultant MPs can set up appointments with ministers who will listen, sometimes with scant patience, to the special pleading, but it takes more than the self-interested to change Government policy. The Gun Lobby did have some success. It targetted its efforts on the members of the standing committee of the Firearms Bill, and the Home Secretary was obliged to concede that compensation should be paid to those who would lose guns by confiscation. But lobbies are stronger, by definition, than are commercial undertakings. A lobby can usually call up the unpaid support of MPs, for example the anti-Abortionists: a firm with an axe to grind, or a product to sell, can call upon its local MP for help, or pay for another to put its case. The trick, if there is one, lies in picking the right MP. Members are usually good judges of other Members. The wrong choice is only too easy to make ('no case was ever finally lost until Mr X made it his own'), and outside bodies can all too often be misled by the reputation of an MP.

I have been a consultant of a different sort. On behalf of an advertising agency I invite prominent politicians to a series of celebrity lunches where they speak off the record to the chairmen and managing directors of the agency's client companies. Success or failure can, at least, be measured. The *prominenti* either turn up or they do not. The success or failure of the more traditional kind of consultancy is much less easy to estimate. I suspect that it is a matter of vanity reinforced and money wasted.

An MP never lacks invitations of one kind or another. Watch a Member, newly arrived in the early afternoon, opening the bundle of his post in the tea room. Letters containing cheques naturally have a special status: so, too, do invitation cards, heavy with embossed lettering, which summon the Tribune to lunch with the French Ambassador or to dine at the Connaught Hotel with the executives of London Weekend Television.

The pink slips are kept to last. On his journey from car park to tea room, the MP has to pass through the Members' Lobby and its letter board. Cheerful attendants hand him pink telephone message slips on which are written instructions to telephone the BBC or to get in touch with the features editor of a great national newspaper. Pink slips are currency of the Realm. They are the means whereby the MP with views, and few of us are entirely without them, can market them most profitably. The winner of the ballot for private members' bills can, if his cause is sufficiently interesting to say nothing of being worthwhile, pick up a pretty penny from the populars. 'Why horses must not be tethered' or 'Page three girls are an insult to my sex' are precisely the subjects of pieces in the populars for which their editors will pay many hundreds of pounds. MPs with heavier views on weighty topics can be invited to explain them in the *Telegraph* or to defend them late at night on 'Newsnight' on BBC2. There are a few MPs who are better known as writers than politicians, and who double their parliamentary salaries by means of their pens. But there is scarcely an MP, however humble, who has not picked up the odd penny in perks. Mr Harry Greenway, a garrulous ex-school teacher, entertains the girls of the Miss World competition to lunch every year.

The achievement of celebrity status by an MP is marked by the arrival in the post of invitations to speak at lunches and dinners, but to do so for money. There are firms such as 'Celebrity Speakers', and 'Prestige Performers' (run by Bernard Braden and Barbara Kelly) which provide horses for lush courses. Recently I have been driven to Gloucester to speak to a sales conference lunch for £1,000. Michael Heseltine, who long ago achieved the rank of celebrity, has been paid as much as £3,000 for a speech, a sum of money which I have only earned on one occasion. Michael is a serious fellow; I am usually invited in order to amuse, a talent which is, if less worthy, still in demand. In April 1989 I journeyed to Weston near Birmingham in order to bring a smile to the tired faces of twenty-two American bankers, and was paid at the rate of £136 a head. It was much more than I deserved but I looked upon the exercise as deferred payment for the hundreds of times I have struggled to village halls to 'address' small audiences of Conservative ladies for absolutely nothing; not even my modest expenses. Humour is in short supply in politics, and it can turn out to be a two-edged weapon as I have found out to my cost. My promotion to the rank of 'celebrity' is probably due to the Radio 4 programme 'Out of Order', a political quiz, which sprung in its turn from the appearance of Austin Mitchell, Charles Kennedy and myself ('Critch, Mitch and Titch') on BBC Radio's 'Today' programme, when we make irreverent comments about the course of politics.

An MP, riding to the Dorchester in a cab on his way to a lunch paid for by some industrialist, can calculate his emoluments on the back of an envelope. His salary of £26,701 a year, now happily linked to that of a senior grade in the Civil Service. As much again in secretarial and research allowances, with no bar to employing his deserving relatives. A London allowance (if his home is out of London) of some £968 a month which he can use to buy a house which is his to sell upon defeat or retirement. A car allowance of nearly 56p a mile, if he drives, as many of us do, a car with an engine of more than 2000cc. A pension of up to 53.6 per cent of the parliamentary salary payable (index linked) to the long-serving and a severance payment, tax free, equal to his final year's salary. And retirement can be taken at 60. None of this is extravagant, but it does provide a most comfortable foundation on which to make money elsewhere. Mrs Thatcher's Britain may recently have adopted Guizot's slogan '*enrichessez-vous*', but MPS have long set a good example.

# 7

# *Gentlemen*

IN MY book *Westminster Blues*, I wrote of the Macmillan years, a time when the Tory party was well suited (dark cloth, Brigade ties and shiny black shoes), and the ambiance still had something of the days of 'Chips' Channon. In 1959, the Tory party was much grander than it has become under Mrs Thatcher. The deferential working class was represented by Mr Ray Mawby, a one-time trade unionist who had been returned for a safe, South Devon seat. With an exquisite act of patronage, Harold Macmillan, grandson of a crofter and kinsman of a duke, promoted Mawby to become Assistant Postmaster General, a post long abandoned which, at that time, might have been described as the dustbin of government.

I found election to the Commons as Member for Rochester at the age of 28 a somewhat daunting experience. Not everyone has the self-confidence of a William Hague who, at 16, obliged Mrs Thatcher to climb to her feet after his speech at a Tory conference. I said little, wrote more and observed a great deal. The Chamber seemed full of heroes, men who had guided the destiny of the nation during the war, or, if they had not been so eminent in that conflict, had rowed across the North Sea single-handed. The Tory benches, in particular, were full of the bemedalled, the more articulate of whom had published an account of their derring-do. Labour MPs were more likely to have served at home, in the ranks of the civil service.

The 1959–64 Parliament was dominated for most of its time by the Prime Minister. Harold Macmillan, who kept his natural anxiety hidden behind a carefully-cultivated pose of unflappability, reached the summit of his powers in 1960. He had rescued the fortunes of government and party after Suez. He had led his party to an unprecedented third election victory running with a level of the popular vote far higher than that to be attained later by Mrs Thatcher in 1987. Macmillan had always been on the 'left' of the party. Indeed, Clement Attlee had once forecast that Macmillan would one day lead the Labour party. In those days radicalism did not mean 'selling off the family silver', as Macmillan himself was later to describe privatisation, but the pursuit of genuinely radical policies such as 'the wind of change', that is withdrawal from empire, and espousal of the cause of Britain in Europe.

I have hung in my drawing room a print of a picture painted in 1960 by A. B. Thomson which was a celebration of Macmillan's election victory. It shows the Prime Minister at the dispatch box during the debate on the Queen's Speech, an occasion when his son Maurice, then the MP for Halifax, moved the Loyal Address. The original hung in Birch Grove, in the corridor outside the dining-room; backbenchers who had been asked to subscribe to the gift of the picture were permitted to buy prints of it at £15 a time. In the picture, Macmillan seems to have the world at his feet. The Tory benches (I am sitting way up on the highest of the backbenches, three away from the young Margaret Thatcher) give off an air of glossy triumph rising almost to a sense of permanence. They clearly did not believe the years to have been wasted. 1960 was still a world in which shirts were white and so were breast-pocket handkerchiefs: coloured shirts and blue silk hankies were fifteen years away.

The past is present in the seated figure of Sir Winston Churchill. Although he was locked into silence by the hardness of his cerebral arteries, his was the brooding presence. He was wheeled into the Chamber twice a week for Prime Minister's Questions, and then, after what appeared to be a superhuman act of levitation, wheeled out again. He was the silent source of Macmillan's power. Had he not once said to Harold that had it not been for Adolf Hitler neither of them would have got to the top in politics? Macmillan, like Sir Anthony Eden, had been with Churchill against Chamberlain and the party's establishment in the 'thirties.

The future is lurking behind the Speaker's chair. The jaunty figure of 'Jolly Jack' Profumo, wearing a curiously light grey suit for his time and place, has evidently dropped in to the Chamber – an interval, I would like to think, between an exquisite light lunch and a tea-time assignation. At the end of the Government front bench, sitting next to the Prime Minister, is Martin Redmayne, the Chief Whip. It was to be Redmayne's incompetence that led, in great part, to the disaster of the Profumo affair of 1963. Harold Macmillan was strangely unworldly when it came to matters of sex, but the whips should not have been as cloistered. A whip must be a man of the world. Whether or not Redmayne and John Hare, the chairman of the party, believed Profumo's protestations of innocence, I do not know, but their reasonable doubts should have been conveyed to the Prime Minister. What otherwise are party whips for?

Opposite the Prime Minister, Hugh Gaitskell is consulting his notes. He was the last high-minded leader of the Labour party. Wilson was a party manager, Callaghan a jovial survivor, Foot a good man out of his place and Neil Kinnock a boy sent on a man's errand. Macmillan and Gaitskell did not like one another, although there was a mutual respect. Gaitskell disliked Macmillan's carefully-cultivated streak of vulgarity, and what he believed to be the Prime Minister's opportunism. Macmillan did not warm to the priggishness of Hugh Gaitskell. It was the clash of two cultures: those of Eton and Winchester.

The figure of Aneurin Bevan is missing, as by November 1960, when the picture was painted, he had recently died of cancer. He made what turned out to be his final major appearance in the House at the end of 1959 when he warned the packed Tory benches that they had little to face save the prospect of 'hours and hours of infinite boredom'. I repeated the message (with due acknowledgement to its author) in the debate on the Queen's Speech immediately after the general election of 1987, thereby incurring the wrath of my constituency party's executive committee who could not understand the purpose of such levity. But party activists are a funny lot; mine most certainly put up with a great deal. The last straw might well have been my invitation to Michael Foot to dine with me at the Gay Hussar in order that I could write about the restaurant in the *Daily Telegraph*. The

President of the Aldershot Conservative Association was not amused. But he has since resigned, ostensibly over a different issue.

I suppose the bulk of those portrayed in Thomson's picture must have died, and by so doing, joined at last the 'great majority'. The ruffians' bench, the Opposition front bench below the gangway, which is today the haunt of the two Dennis's, Skinner and Canavan, was occupied in November 1960 by a group of formidable iconoclasts. Desmond Donelley who was later to kill himself in a hotel bedroom, Emrys Hughes who had a huge capacity for parliamentary mischief, Mrs Bessie Braddock, the political 'boss' of the pre-Militant Liverpool party machine, and Sidney Silverman, the best barrack-room lawyer in the business, whose duels on points of order with the Speaker, Harry Hylton-Foster, were a joy to watch. In the 'eighties, the Government benches below the gangway are the home of Tory ruffians who, unlike Labour backbenchers, tend to hunt in packs. In 1960, the front bench was occupied by Winston Churchill (who sits in the place which is today reserved for Edward Heath) and a string of fairly distinguished lawyers who can be identified by their uniform of black jacket and trousers.

In 1960, the two best speakers in the Commons were Michael Foot and Nigel Birch. Foot was the great radical tribune who appeared to be anchored on the Labour backbenches. In turn passionate and witty, his dialectic was a powerful weapon deployed against what he saw to be the vulgarity and boneheadedness of the Government. Foot is a great platform orator; his style brings to the Commons echoes of past and present discontents: of Chartism, of mass unemployment and of the dangers of an undue reliance upon nuclear weapons. Nigel Birch was very different. He was an assassin. He had the kind of sardonic wit which could delight like a fine white Burgundy, and which at the same time was like acid that could strip the skin from the backs of his enemies. He rarely made a speech that lasted for more than ten minutes, but he made every second count. His target was Harold Macmillan and what he believed to be the Prime Minister's profligacy. He had, of course, resigned as a Treasury minister in 1958, along with the then Chancellor, Peter Thorneycroft and Enoch Powell, in protest against an increase in public spending. His gesture had been dismissed by Harold Macmillan who left the next morning for Australia, as 'a little local difficulty', an act of political insouciance which amounted to genius. Birch never forgot his humiliation, and nor did he forgive.

By 1962, the Macmillan magic was beginning to fade. The Prime Minister dismissed a third of his cabinet overnight, and replaced Selwyn Lloyd as Chancellor with the more expansionist minded Reginald Maudling. Birch wrote a memorable letter to *The Times*. 'For the second time, the Prime Minister has got rid of a Chancellor of the Exchequer who tried to get expenditure under control. Once is more than enough.' In 1963, when the Profumo scandal broke, it was Birch who emerged as a willing Cassandra. I shall never forget his speech in the Profumo debate on 17 June 1963. I sat immediately behind the Prime Minister on a seat above the gangway traditionally occupied by the party's loyalists. Birch spoke from below the gangway.

I think it not too much to say that Birch's speech destroyed Macmillan. He contrived to be contemptuous of John Profumo, but much more contemptuous of a Government which had not seen through Profumo. 'I must say that he never struck me at all as a man like a cloistered monk, and Miss Keeler was a professional prostitute. There seems to me to be a certain basic improbability about the proposition that their conduct was purely platonic.'

In fact, Miss Keeler was not 'a professional prostitute', but in any case she got off relatively lightly from Birch. For him the real culprit was Macmillan for permitting it all to have come about. He did not suggest that the Prime Minister had acted dishonourably, but 'on the question of competence and good sense I cannot think that the verdict can be favourable'. It was time, continued Birch, twisting his knife in the wound, for Macmillan 'to make way for a younger colleague'. Birch's peroration was from Browning's 'The Lost Leader'. 'Let him never come back to us', the quotation began, and ended, 'never glad confident morning again'.

As Birch delivered his final line, Macmillan turned towards him, his face contorted with pain and anger. It remains an indelible impression upon my memory. For Birch, the Profumo affair was no little, local difficulty. Revenge was sweet.

In the Thatcher years the Tory party was rent by the conflict between the Prime Minister's desire for radical change, and those Tories who did not share her enthusiasms and who disliked her style: the famous battle between the 'wets' and the 'arditi', the ardent ones whose liberalism owed more to Manchester than to Hampstead. In the 'sixties, the Tory party was riven by the conflict between Macmillan and his right wing. Harold Macmillan had already laid himself open to attack from the right over his Commonwealth policy. He had journeyed to Africa and told the South African parliament that 'the wind of change' was sweeping across their continent. It is hard now to remember that when Macmillan took office in 1957, a large part of Africa was ruled from Whitehall. Decolonialisation seemed inevitable, but Macmillan was never forgiven by the party's diehards for the speed with which he set about dismantling the Empire – a task which he placed in the hands of another moderate, progressive Tory, Iain Macleod. In the 'eighties I was no longer a party loyalist: in the 'sixties I was probably the last.

Iain Macleod was the lost leader of the progressive Tories. He was anathema to the old, traditionalist right, as typified by Julian Amery, Sir Patrick Wall and Sir John Biggs-Davison. 'Too clever by half' was Lord Salisbury's description of him. His other sin was youth; he was the youngest member of Macmillan's cabinet. He was the Tory most feared by the Labour party. 'Much the most intelligent member of the stupid party', Michael Foot wrote of him. At his oratorical best, Macleod could sweep all before him, with a powerful mixture of passion, humour and intellect.

His was a brooding presence on any political platform. He sat hunched. His back disability, an unusual form of arthritis, made worse by a war injury, made it impossible for him to turn his neck. (It prevented him from driving a motor-car.) It meant that he was in almost constant pain but suffering gave him an air of unyielding stolidity which made his many qualities seem all the more impressive. He had one of the quickest minds in the House, honed by years of playing top-class bridge. He was one of the group of four players who had invented the Acol system: before the war he was said to have netted £2,000 a year tax free from his winnings at bridge. He was for years a professional gambler, as much as any river boat gambler who plied the Mississippi at the turn of the century, playing poker. He had a prodigious memory. His biographer, Nigel Fisher, records that 'he knew the whole of T. S. Eliot by heart'.

To many of us, Iain Macleod was the obvious successor to Harold Macmillan. But it was Lord Home who 'emerged' from the chaos which surrounded Macmillan's resignation in October 1963. This showed how important it was in the Conservative party not so much to have a body of devoted supporters as it was not to have a section of the party hostile towards you: Macleod and his policies had antagonised too many Conservative MPs; he was too controversial a figure in a party in which a safe pair of hands was still considered the highest form of political praise.

In Thomson's picture, Edward Heath can be distinguished sitting on the front bench. Ted Heath had managed to build for himself a very considerable reputation inside the House while being, at that time, largely unknown outside it. He had been the most formidable Chief Whip the party had known this century, steering the Tories through the Suez crisis. A Chief Whip does not cut a figure with the public at large; and there are times when he can become less than popular with his fellow MPs, but chief whips are accorded a peculiar respect within the Tory party, a fact which can be accounted for, so cynics might say, because there is a certain sort of Englishman who feels most comfortable when deferring to anyone in authority; the school prefect syndrome. Ted Heath was the head prefect *par excellence*.

Macmillan had picked Macleod to do his bidding over Africa. By the same token he chose Heath to further his aims in Europe. In 1960 he had the title of Lord Privy Seal. His responsibility was to negotiate Britain's entry into the European Common Market. This task involved enormously hard, detailed work. It called for great patience and the ability to explain the complexities in layman's language. His mastery of kangaroo meat earned him the nickname 'the Grocer', which his enemies employed throughout his premiership. His skills typified the managerial approach to politics which became fashionable later in the 'sixties, and his toughness and courage in identifying and then overcoming a raft of vested interest laid the foundations for his triumph in 1972 when, as Prime Minister, he took Britain into Europe.

After de Gaulle's veto in January 1963, Heath was promoted to the formidably titled office of 'Secretary of state for Industry, Trade and Regional Development and President of the Board of Trade'. The post went to the heart of the internal affairs of state. Ted Heath never then, nor later, underestimated the part that governments must play in fostering industry and trade and in keeping the balance between regions within Britain. But he was also engaged in trying to persuade the party to rediscover the importance of market economics. As Trade Secretary he was responsible for the abolition of retail price maintenance. This measure proved to be the most controversial of Sir Alec Douglas-Home's government, and its importance is hard for people today to understand. It was not until the reform was passed in 1964 that shops could compete against one another on prices on branded goods. There was to be, and at long last, the ability to shop around for the best buy. The shopkeeper interests opposed the bill strongly, as I discovered in Rochester and Chatham, and shopkeepers made up the bulk of local Conservative constituency party executive committees. The free market right of the Tory party that today is pre-eminent would do well to remember Ted's liberal antecedents.

Ted Heath was never a sparkling parliamentary performer, but he was painstaking and competent. He did not make mistakes. He forced through the abolition of retail price maintenance largely by force of character. Who can say whether his Act helped or hindered at the election of October 1964? Mr Wilson's majority was wafer thin. Nevertheless, Heath's reward came in 1965 when he was elected the leader of the party. He was judged by his colleagues to be more likely to provide robust opposition to Harold Wilson than his rival, Reginald Maudling. And he had succeeded where the more charismatic Iain Macleod had failed. Iain did not let his name go forward at the Tory party's leadership election.

In my picture the Government backbenches contain many of the now barely recognisable. Christopher Chataway, fit and gingery, a world-class athlete who had consolidated his fame as a television news reader and personality. It was not long before he was made a minister, but he quit politics eventually for the lusher pastures of merchant banking. Humphry Berkeley, who can lay claim to have been the most productive backbencher since A. P. Herbert, is in the frame. He took up the cause of homosexual law reform and succeeded in changing the law, and with it, public attitudes. He also was the prime mover in breaking the 'magic circle' out of which leaders of the Conservative party had long 'emerged'. He was never popular with 'the colleagues'. His views were anathema to most of us (not to me), and his sharp tongue and prickly disposition was widely feared. He was no respecter of the old and not-so-bold, the 'silly old things' who made up, and still do, the chorus of the Tory party. He lost his seat at Lancaster in '66, since which time he has shopped around the other political parties, but without much success. A talent lost to politics by the party system.

Margaret Thatcher had been elected in 1959. She too swiftly became a junior minister, promoted by Martin Redmayne after her successful private members' bill permitting the press to attend council meetings. A primitive Conservative, her views were unfashionably fundamentalist, and widely disregarded by her peers. Later to become one of the great comic figures of our time (or so thinks Mr Neil Kinnock), in 1960 she was yet another ambitious newly elected Tory MP, a woman who was generally avoided by her more sophisticated, and ultimately less successful, colleagues. I should, of course, have recognised her as a force of nature, but I did not.

The painting contains several of the 'lads' who, in Housman's words, 'would never grow old'. Peter Kirk who was to die in the 'seventies of a heart attack, knighted for his services to Britain in Europe, a man whose natural talent might have led him to the topmost rank of politics. And David Walder, barrister, novelist, historian, wit and politician who died suddenly in 1978, succumbing to a second heart attack. He had been a whip in Ted Heath's government, and was universally popular. He had no time for Margaret. I doubt whether he would have flourished after 1979.

Among the more senior figures were Brigadier Anthony Head, who was later to be sent as High Commissioner to Nigeria by the Prime Minister, and Fitzroy Maclean, arguably Britain's finest fighting soldier of the Second World War, the author of *Eastern Approaches* and a junior minister in Churchill's post-war government. He was knighted eventually, but he should be in the Lords.

91

His wife wrote one of the most successful cookery books in the language. It is a superb blend of snobbery and gastronomy for she stumbled on the idea of writing to all her friends in great houses and asking them to send her their favourite menus written upon their own writing paper. The letters were then published as written – by the best cooks in the employ of the British upper classes.

Does distance lend enchantment? The minor actors on the Westminster stage seemed to have more sparkle than their counterparts do today. Among the awkward squad was the splendid figure of 'Hinch', Lord Hinchingbrooke. He hated the Common Market. He resembled, monocle in eye, a figure from a Wodehouse novel, but he usually managed to say something of interest. 'Hinch' was no silly ass. He disclaimed his title, but by that time it was too late; try as he did he could not manage to be returned to the Commons as plain Mr Victor Montagu. The commander of the party's awkward squad was Sir Gerald Nabarro whose handle-bar moustache was as much a trademark as Hinch's eye-glass. Self-made and accident prone, he was the universal radio and television panellist with a line in right-wing populism which anticipated the fashions of today. Yet he was a formidable operator who managed, thanks to homework well done, to get the better of many a tongue-tied junior minister. His campaign to reveal the lunacies of purchase tax was ultimately successful. He once gave me tea at his house in Broadway. As I sat in his study I counted sixty-six photographs or cartoons of my host displayed upon the walls. A more loveable figure was Sir Godfrey Nicholson whose interventions were never predictable. When he gave up his seat in Farnham in 1970, the town council placed a bust of him in the park within earshot of a pub called 'The William Cobbett'. The bust fell victim to the pub's drunken customers, but in compensation his daughter Emma was elected to the Commons in 1987.

Jo Grimond is in the picture, leaning forward, notes in hand. Grimond is an immensely attractive man with a flair for the elegant, minor contribution. It was his style to come in after the two front bench speakers and gently point out that, in fact, neither emperor was properly dressed. He belonged, as benefitted a grandson-in-law of Herbert Asquith, to a more spacious, civilised and elegant age of politics, yet he never gave the appearance of being out of date. But the strain of leading a party which won millions of votes but invariably ended up with half a dozen seats because too much of a bore, and he handed over the leadership of the Liberals to Jeremy Thorpe in 1967.

The Government front bench contains several volcanoes. Duncan Sandys (can his hair ever have been that shade of red?) who had been succeeded as Minister of Defence by Harold Watkinson who was, without doubt, the most boring man in the House of Commons. Sandys was the right-wing complement to Iain Macleod over Africa; the one worrying about the Colonies and the other the Commonwealth. Sandys developed two loves later in his political life: Europe and the environment. He served both of them well. Henry Brooke whose decency did not save him from the ridicule of 'That Was the Week That Was'. Ernest Marples, a self-made self-publicist who helped Harold Macmillan build 300,000 tatty houses on windy estates at the end of bus rides on the fringes of Northern industrial towns. Reginald Bevins who was Postmaster General and was to lose his seat and thus his place in the pecking order of advancement. Charles Hill, the one-time Radio Doctor, who was the best platform speaker in the Tory party. And the curved figure of 'Rab' Butler, as eliptical in utterance, whose ambition was to be finally thwarted by a bed-ridden Harold Macmillan who preferred first Hogg and then Home. Butler was almost as much a target for the spite of the unreconstructed Tories as was his rival Harold Macmillan. He was too cerebral for the party stalwart. He had none of Macmillan's style (which many claimed to have seen through years ago), and his war had been far less distinguished. His work in bringing the party political up to date in the years immediately after 1945 was recognised but not admired. He had the tendency to see more than one side of the question, a failing from which Mrs Thatcher has never suffered. Among the young Conservative MPS he had a devoted following, but when it came to the premiership the 'magic circle' cast its malign spell. When he had to fight his corner 'Rab' never seemed to want anything badly enough.

I am fond of my print of Thomson's picture. It is the first of two snapshots of the House of Commons, taken in my time. The other (in fact, two pictures were painted by different artists as the first was not large enough to accommodate all MPS and the *refusés* clubbed together and had themselves a second picture painted) was done in 1987. Now that Birch Grove has been sold out of the Macmillan family, I do not know what has happened to the original of Thomson's picture. Perhaps the second Earl of Stockton has found room for it? The originals of the other two pictures hang in the Strangers' Dining Room of the Commons, a cheerful accompaniment to the hospitality of MPS and the appetites of wives, mothers and constituents.

Among the host of parliamentary spear carriers, many stand out. Bill Yates, the Tory MP for the Wrekin, a passionate Arabist who would parade through the streets of Wellington on election night wearing desert dress. He was known by the irreverent as 'Mohammed El Ya Tees' and was widely regarded as delightful and dotty. He eventually left Westminster for a seat in the Australian Federal Parliament. George Wigg, cantankerous and vindictive, who pursued Profumo to the kill. He came into his own later when he served as dogsbody to a paranoid Harold Wilson. Sir Jocelyn Lucas who looked like Macmillan and bred Sealyham dogs; he was a great disapprover of the dress of his fellows, his disapproval for suede shoes being particularly marked.

So many of the Tories were knighted that it became easier to spot those who were not. Under Harold Macmillan, a Tory backbencher of ten years' service was almost always knighted; twelve years merited a baronetcy. Ted Heath took a more austere view, as one might expect from one who had supported the Republic in the Spanish civil war. His parsimony with awards helped to sap his personal popularity. After Mrs Thatcher became leader of the party, I asked her at lunch whether she was likely to continue in the Heathian tradition. 'Certainly not' was her reply, and she has certainly lived up to her boast. Under Margaret a 'K' stands ready for any backbencher who has served his time, has not cheeked the Prime Minister, or taken care to tell the whips that he is not interested.

# 8

# *Players*

IN RECENT years the *Spectator*, that venerable political weekly, has given a lunch at the Savoy Hotel for politicians and political journalists. The purpose was public relations. A Scotch whisky company, one of the magazine's many owners, paid the bill; the editor of the *Spectator* presented his annual awards to parliamentarians (the jury consisted of political writers) and a very good time was had by all. It was the best free lunch in London as one might have expected from a peccable right-wing weekly. A hundred guests sat at separate tables, politicians of the best sort and newspaper and television political journalists, the top table was reserved for cabinet ministers, editors and a Gaelic paymaster.

Awards are fun. There is the *Spectator*'s 'Parliamentarian of the Year', which in 1988 went to Edward Heath for his frequent and adversely critical attacks on the policies of Mrs Thatcher's Administration. This was a handsome gesture on the part of the jury, a gesture which was spoilt by a predictable attack on Ted Heath in the editorial columns of the magazine. We should have become used to that sort of attack, favoured by the right wing, along the lines that the former Tory leader was motivated solely by rancour and spite, having failed to come to terms with his defeat in the leadership election of 1975. Heath and Thatcher do not like one another, but the charge that repels is ideological. They stand for distinctly different strands in the Conservative tradition.

The *Spectator* awards include that of the 'Backbencher of the Year'. This has gone, in the past, to mavericks such as Nicholas Budgen, the Tory MP for Wolverhampton South West, and Enoch

Powell's successor. Budgen, who is witty, gregarious, excitable (he has only to sniff a glass in the smoking room to be on the top of his form) and pithy, was once a Tory whip. But he is not one of nature's policemen. He quit, and by so doing probably ruined his chances of ministerial office. Once a lawyer and now a journalist, he rides to hounds, as did Enoch, but his quarry is not just the Midlands fox; he is a cheerful put-downer of ministerial humbug, and no worshipper at the altar of the Great Ones of the party. He has given the Government backbenches a good name.

Tam Dalyell has also won the award. Tam is an awkward customer. A Scots 'gent', and a Tory when at Oxford, Dalyell has pursued Mrs Thatcher, and her failings, with zeal. He is the Moby Dick to her Great White Whale. In search of what he sees as the truth about Mrs Thatcher's part in the Westland affair, Dalyell has been frequently suspended from sittings of the Commons. He is physically somewhat uncoordinated. I was once sitting in the Central Lobby in the company of, I believe, Sir Spencer Summers, a Tory MP of the old school. Together, and in silence, we watched Dalyell enter the lobby, walk across it and disappear in the direction of the real world. 'If he were a horse', said Sir Spencer, 'I wouldn't buy him.' Tam might not have made a racehorse, but he is no mean stayer. Honest, obstinate, and eccentric, Tam is a credit to the faintly disreputable trade of politics.

Dennis Skinner, the 'beast' of Bolsover, is another Westminster original. He has made a career out of insult. He was once described to me by Phillip Whitehead, at the time a Labour MP for Derby, as being 'much the nicest of the seven Skinner brothers', and I knew exactly what he meant. My admiration for Dennis's iconoclasm was tempered early in 1989 when he spoke at a meeting of the Yateley Labour party in my constituency. He accused me of 'neglecting my constituency' on the grounds that I wrote articles for magazines, and worked for a private company. (Presumably he meant that I was public affairs advisor to SSC&B Lintas, an advertising agency.) Skinner, who has a Cromwellian attitude to MPs' pay, believing that we should all do as he does and draw only the average industrial wage, tends to judge his colleagues on that score. He is entitled to his view, and there is indeed something admirable about his self-denial, but to make an offensive attack on an opponent's competence (as opposed to his views) on such flimsy grounds, tells us something about Skinner. Is writing for magazines such a grievous sin? If so, what about Roy Hattersley: has he not comforted a generation of dental patients with his pieces in *Punch*? Has Roy neglected his constituency? It is more than my life is worth to enter into the quarrels of the parliamentary Labour party: it is enough to say that Skinner has become the past master at the sedentary interruption and the parliamentary insult, and a major Westminster character. Yet underneath all that coal dust must beat a heart of gold.

The *Spectator* once gave an award for the 'Troublemaker of the Year', but the apple was not altogether a welcome gift. Constituency parties tended to view the award of such a prize to their Tory MP with embarrassment. Tories are not elected to Parliament to cause trouble, not, that is, to their own side. Jonathan Aitken is a Tory troublemaker, one of the best. Jonathan is a romantically-inclined right winger, and the great-nephew of Lord Beaverbrook. Handsome, fluent and brave, he is one Tory MP who does not give a damn. His bonnet buzzes with bees: official secrecy – he was once prosecuted unsuccessfully under the Official Secrets Act at the time of the Biafran war – the iniquity of the European Community (echoes of Max Beaverbrook's espousal of the lost cause of Empire) and the undesirability of the Channel Tunnel. Had his affair with Carole Thatcher lasted, he might have become 'one of us' in a way that not even Mr Cecil Parkinson could claim to be. His business career has been as stormy as it has been successful – who can forget Anna Ford's gesture at the time of the troubles of TV AM when she turned the water into wine?

In 1987 a second portrait was painted of the House of Commons in session by Grace Mendoza. It shows a packed House in which a shaft of sunlight falls tactfully upon the Prime Minister, whose mood, if we are to judge from her expression, is uncharacteristically benign. She is more likely to be under fire. I have descended three benches in thirty years, and am seated crushed between Sir William Clark, another 'fifty-niner', whose loyalty to party and Government is a by-word, and Mr Patrick Cormack, whose frock-coated presence has lent tone to many a St Margaret's Memorial Service. At my present rate of progress it will be the year 2017 before I will be discovered crouched on the front bench below the gangway. Miss Mendoza is a charitable painter who has put her subjects in the best of lights. When the idea of the portrait was first discussed, I did suggest that John Bratby be asked to undertake the task. But we politicians, who go to Westminster in order to avoid the kitchen sink, are nothing if not vain. We are not in favour of warts.

John Biffen sits on the Government front bench. He was still then the Leader of the House, although he had been described by Mr Bernard Ingham on behalf of his mistress, as being 'semi-detached'. This rebuke had been earned prior to the '87 election by Biffen's famous call on Midlands television for 'a balanced ticket', by which he presumably meant that we should see less of Mrs Thatcher and more of her ministers. It seemed reasonable enough at the time. John Biffen is perhaps the most attractive of Tory politicians. The son of a Somerset dirt-farmer, John was brought up in Bridgwater. He went to Cambridge where he got a First, and then into politics, winning a by-election in 1961 at Oswestry, a Welsh-speaking railway town just this side of the Shropshire border.

Under Ted Heath, Biffen was kept locked up on the backbenches. He was a nationalist and a disciple of Enoch Powell. Under Margaret his career blossomed, only to wither as he came to dislike her 'self-righteousness' and her display of armoured simplicity. In the jargon of the mid 'eighties, he became a 'consolidator', anxious lest the pace of the counter-revolution outrun the support of the electorate. He ought not to have worried. The lesson of the 'eighties is surely that change, whereas it may not always be welcomed, is accepted for as long as the living standards of the majority are seen to rise. John was effectively squeezed out of the inner counsels of Mrs Thatcher's second administration, and upon her victory in 1987 was promptly sacked. He was the best Leader of the House since the war. Witty and polite, his performances, in a role which demands the good will of MPs of all political parties, were invariably a pleasure. He has said that he is not in business to make life easy for Mrs Thatcher, and he is not the sort to break a promise. He is not seen as a contender for the leadership of the party; he is too diffident, too 'un-physical' for the demands of the highest office. What is certain is that he will return to the cabinet under her successor. In the meantime John will continue to give politics a good name.

Mr Cranley Onslow is seated high up on the Government backbenches. His is not a household name. As the chairman of the 1922 Committee of Tory backbenchers, he is as important politically as the Government Chief Whip. The '22 meets every Thursday evening at 6 p.m. in Committee Room 14. It elects its officers and executive committee annually. Cranley Onslow replaced Edward du Cann as the party's 'shop steward'. It has been Cranley's policy to be as unlike his predecessor as possible. Where du Cann, a former chairman of the party, and leadership contender at the time of the Peasants' Revolt, enjoyed much publicity, Onslow keeps his silence. He was not prepared to talk to me in 1989 when I wrote a profile of him for the *Observer* newspaper.

Onslow is a Tory 'gent' of traditional right-wing views. He travels in integrity. Tough and combative, although invariably courteous in his dealings with 'the colleagues', he enjoys, as does his executive committee, immediate access to the Prime Minister. He is certainly not afraid of her as many Tories are. It was he who told Mrs Thatcher in January 1986 that Leon Brittan should go. He carried to her the message of a hostile '22. The executive holds regular meetings with the Prime Minister, and should Cranley wish to see the Chief Whip, the latter's desk would be swiftly cleared. The individual Conservative backbencher may count for little: anyone who can claim to speak on behalf of all 250 is a heavyweight indeed.

Mrs Thatcher's political strength derives not only from her ability to deliver electoral success, but from the rapport which she enjoys with the bulk of her backbenchers. She has sat upon the Peacock Throne so long that the waves of new entry have come in part to take up the colour of her style and prejudices. We are, after all, a right-wing political party. All Prime Ministers are obliged to watch their backs. Mr Harold Macmillan's relationship with his backbenchers was, at best, equivocal, at worst one of mutual distrust. Sir Alec basked in their affection, if not always enjoying their respect. Ted Heath permitted his position to be undermined through his neglect of the '22 Committee. In 1975, when his leadership was challenged by election, the chairman and

officers of the '22 behaved like so many colonels in the Portu-
guese revolution, parading the corridors upstairs with rifles in the
muzzles of which were stuck the roses of disaffection. Mrs
Thatcher has not made Ted Heath's mistake. She has kept in
touch with the '22, sweetening its members with knighthoods on
behalf of Her Majesty the Queen. She survived the capture of the
Falklands and the haroosh of the Westland affair. Her relationship with Cranley Onslow and his executive, which includes
moderates such as Sir Charles Morrison and Sir Geoffrey Johnson Smith, is one which she take care to keep in good repair.

Cranley Onslow is a kinsman of the Earl of Onslow, and the
family's name is blazoned over much of West Surrey. Every
garage seems to be called 'Onslow Motors'. He has been a
minister of state at the Foreign and Commonwealth Office, and
he resigned that office when his boss, Francis Pym, was discharged by Mrs Thatcher immediately after her victory in '83. He
has old-fashioned views about loyalty. He is gingery, arthritic,
robust and humorous. Nobody has a keener eye for the absurdi-
ties of his colleagues.

Mr Douglas Hurd sits on the Government front bench. I have
always thought there is a touch of the schoolmaster about Hurd.
He reminds me of the sort of prep school headmaster who would
have been introduced into the school mid-term by the Governing
body in order to bring the school round after a disastrous period
of disorder. He has a hint of the cold baths about him. As Home
Secretary he was obliged to come between the backbenches and
their hearts' desire, the return of the rod and the rope. He would
be unlikely to succeed the Prime Minister as leader of the party
for as long as our leaders are elected and do not 'emerge' as they
once did. Twenty-five years ago Mr Iain Macleod, writing in the
*Spectator*, succeeded in changing the rules. Were they ever to be
reversed, and the 'magic circle' reconstituted, then Douglas could
come into his own.

Imagine the scene. Lord Whitelaw would have invited leading
Tories to dine at White's. They would eat oysters, bloody beef
and semolina pudding in the midst of which would nestle a dollop
of strawberry jam. They would drink several bottles of a decent
claret such as Cheval Blanc '61. ('No dark horse in this bottle,'
says Willie). After some vintage port the cabal would get down to

business. 'Shall I begin', says Willie, 'by asking whether Douglas would let his name go forward?' The Home Secretary's record would be solemnly rehearsed. Unanimously he would be accorded 'bottom', that mysterious quality without which no Tory can succeed at anything. The diners would be reminded that he had been Captain of Pop at Eton. He was clearly a better sort of Tory who would provide a Safe Pair of Hands.

A voice might have been raised in favour of George Younger, but the weight of the meeting would incline remorselessly in favour of Douglas. At 1 a.m., when the bar of White's closes and after a word in the hall with Julian Amery in order to learn the view of the man in the street, the party would, at Lord Whitelaw's bidding, go down the road to Pratt's. At Pratt's, over a nightcap, agreement would be reached. After three puffs of smoke, Willie would telephone Douglas at home. 'Douglas? Willie here. I have bad news for you.' 'Oh God,' thinks Hurd, pyjama'd but without his spectacles. 'We want you to lead our great party.' The circle would then summon cabs but not before a message had been passed down the street to the members of the Carlton. 'A courtesy only,' says Whitelaw. Since they amalgamated with the Junior Carlton they are all in bed at 10 o'clock.

Before an unexpected cabinet reshuffle granted Hurd the Foreign Office, his prospects were murky. As Foreign Secretary, Geoffrey Howe could travel the world tidying up after Mrs Thatcher. Kenneth Baker could always publish a new anthology of verse. Michael Heseltine could eat rubber chicken uninvited at a thousand constituency dinners, and Norman Tebbit's pen could put money in the hands of lawyers. Douglas had little to look forward to, save for the annual seaside humiliations of the Conservative party conference. With his high intelligence and moderate views he should make an extremely able Foreign Secretary.

In the leadership contest, the Tory moderates would suffer from an *embarras de choix*. Mr Kenneth Baker, the Jack Buchanan of our party, is sleek, witty and charmingly flexible. Someone said of him that 'he can strut sitting down'. His Great Education Reform Bill (Gerbil) rationalised the syllabus. He was obliged by Mrs Thatcher to include provisions for the opting out of schools from local education authority control, hijacked by bands of aggrieved parents. I doubt whether many schools will take advantage of the proposal.

101

Mr Michael Heseltine is confident that the Peacock Throne will be his for the taking. He is perhaps the best equipped of the contenders: sharp-witted, handsome and tireless. Early in 1990, he made his bid to take Mrs Thatcher's place. Or, to be more accurate, the newspapers suddenly ran him as Mrs Thatcher's most likely successor. In the previous November, the Prime Minister had been challenged for the leadership of the Tory party by a relatively obscure Tory backbencher, Sir Anthony Meyer, who in the course of a lively campaign picked up a total of 60 votes or abstentions. Mrs Thatcher was privately livid: in public, having done much the same thing to Edward Heath in 1975, she had no choice but put her best face forward. And did not the party's rules permit an annual election? Anthony Meyer cast himself as the stalking horse, but it was Michael Heseltine (who abstained from voting, as I did) who stood to gain from her humiliation.

The public opinion polls moved remorselessly against the Government, and, when the poll tax was introduced in the spring of 1990, the gap between Labour and the Tories widened to more than 20 per cent. Seventy per cent of the voters wanted Mrs Thatcher to stand down before the next election: of the contenders to succeed her, Michael Heseltine was the clear favourite.

But was he the favourite of Tory MPs who do, after all, make up the electorate? At the time of writing he has been careful not to put it to the test. He knows perfectly well that a direct challenge would be savagely contested, and would serve to rally the party loyalists to the Premier's somewhat tattered banner. And even were he to win, it might turn out to be a Pyrrhic victory. He could find difficulty in forming a government; and the residue of bitterness might sour his term of office. Mrs Thatcher gives no sign of wanting to call it a day, and as no lady is ever a gentleman, it would be foolish to rely upon her finer feeling. Were the ship to sink with all hands, she would be glimpsed on the bridge, right hand to the peak of her cap. In the meantime, Heseltine, who is by far the best equipped Tory to succeed her, has to bide his time, and bite his lip. He is fated to campaign ceaselessly by eating lunch with Tory women where he takes care not to mention the Prime Minister by name and attacks robustly the Labour alternative. He is the prisoner of the rubber chicken circuit. The strain of so much hospitality must surely begin to tell.

Having taken Michael Hesletine up, the press – or a good part of it including Murdoch's *Times* and Conrad Black's *Telegraph* – promptly dropped him, preferring, or so it seemed, the devil we knew. The local government election results in early May 1990 proved to be a turning point of sorts. They were far from good from the Government's point of view (they could be translated by the psephologists into a Labour majority at a general election of fifty), but not quite the disaster we feared. Kenneth Baker snatched 'victory' from defeat, thanks to the Conservatives holding Wandsworth and Westminster, (but not Bradford). Mrs Thatcher breathed again. But were the Conservatives to lose the next election, Michael Heseltine would swiftly be elected Leader of the Party. Were we to win a fourth general election victory running, then I fear he will have missed the bus. That famous back of an envelope, on which he scribbled in 1952 while sitting in a restaurant in Oxford the positions he would reach in each of the decades of the century (1990 – 10 Downing street), would have betrayed him.

I have already mentioned Douglas Hurd. In a more gracious age he would have been the choice of the party's establishment. One thing is certain: he has done well to escape from the Home Office, an office of state destined to thwart the strongest-held desires of simpler Conservatives. But we should not overlook Mr Kenneth Clarke. The public may not be entirely convinced that he National Health Service is safe in Mrs Thatcher's hands, and for as long as she refuses to make use of it, who can blame it. Clarke, on the other hand, is a public sector Tory. He is both able, in the sense of being a good administrator, and clever. He has the happy knack of being able to disguise his cleverness, which he does in part by a studied scruffiness and in part by parliamentary good manners. If he is a touch overweight, then there are few Tory MPs who are not. The blame can be put upon Mr Charles Irving, the Chairman of the Kitchen Committee. He will even wear suede shoes, and it must be said that Clarke's suede shoes have acquired over the years a patina of their own. I once ran into him at Queen's Park Rangers' football ground near White City. We were watching Barry McGuigan winning the world featherweight title. I sat in the ringside seats, next to large men with neckties: Clarke, who was at that time a minister of the crown, took his seat in the section of the crowd reserved for McGuigan's Catholic Irish supporters. He lived to tell the tale, blending perfectly as he did with his surroundings.

In time, John Major threatens to become a contender. He is the son of a trapeze artist and has inherited something of his father's skill upon the high wire of politics. He is perhaps a shade to the right of Clarke, his numeracy having led him into the Treasury. His father fell upon hard times, and the Majors lived on the top floor of a large Victorian house in Brixton. The young Major sought his first job at the age of 16 as a bus conductor. There were three candidates for the job: an Irishman who was swiftly eliminated, a West Indian woman and the future Chancellor of the Exchequer. The survivors were given a test of mental arithmetic and physical dexterity. Major won the first test of mental arithmetic but lost the second, and the West Indian woman was duly taken on. Major had a long, sad walk back home late at night from the LTB garage. He later became a labourer and then found his feet in the world of banking. Elected to Parliament in 1979, he is the first of his generation to have entered the cabinet. His rise has been apparently effortless: the Whips' Office, the Department of Health and Social Security and the Treasury. Unlike John Macgregor who threatened to come between the British and their camembert, John Major has led a charmed life, his only secret fear being that he will suffer the fate of John Moore, a former favourite-to-succeed who, like Icarus, flew too close to the sun. Mrs Thatcher is as jealous as Jehovah.

Were Labour to lose the next election, Neil Kinnock would call it a day. I suppose he would be succeeded by John Smith, who is the very best kind of Scottish lawyer. Smith has *gravitas*. He is also flanked by several very promising Labour MPs: John Cunningham, Gordon Brown (yet another Scot), Tony Blair and Robin Cook. But they are all serious people, the subject of *Observer* profiles, and frequent performers on television.

More interesting, if less well known, are people like Alan Clark, the Tory MP for Plymouth who lives in a castle in Kent. Clark has style. As a minister at the Department of Trade and Industry, he remained 'semi-detached' while a member of Her Majesty's Government. I once ran into him at the Tate. In answer to my question as to which picture he had come to see, he told me that he had come to sell the gallery one of his own. The son of Lord Clark of *Civilisation*, Alan is the kind of Tory that gives right wingers a good name: he is literate; witty and independent-minded. In many ways it is a pity he took office. He is kept under ministerial lock and key. He would be much more fun as a *franc-tireur* on the backbenches, pointing the finger of scorn at the vanities of our masters and mistresses.

When I cannot sleep I count backbenchers jumping over fences. It is an act of desperation brought on by the remorseless chiming of known clocks. Geoffrey Dickens in pusuit of a child-molester, Harry Greenway looking for the contestants of Miss World, Julian Brazier, the head boy in search of the headmaster, Nicholas Baker, the family solicitor, Eric Heffer whose nature is as good as his fuse is short, Charles Kennedy carrying the burden of much promise, Sir Raymond Gower as old as the Welsh hills, Sir Michael Shaw for whom no boarding-house door in Scarborough remains shut, Sir Trevor Skeet who resembles my prep school headmaster, Hugh Dykes, another Tory in perpetual opposition to the temper of the times, Sir William Clark who is as loyal as a hound dog, and John Gorst who has 'Grunwick' tattooed on his arm. As the long line of politicians moves towards the fence, each becomes more supple and less recognisable.

When it comes to practising politics many of us never lose our amateur status. The real pros, the professionals who practise the black arts of politics, use their skills to climb the ladder of promotion and, when they have done so, to stay at the top. The amateurs stay on the backbenchers, listlessly playing at politics. Among the pros, Peter Walker is pre-eminent. Michael Heseltine, who is no mean politician himself, has confessed that he learnt all he knows at Walker's knee.

After Mrs Thatcher's third election victory in 1987, she offered Walker Wales. It was a demotion; even a humiliation. A lesser man would have refused, and returned unwillingly to the back-benches to sit high up among the arrivistes, garagistes and clapped-out volcanoes of our party. But Walker preferred to stay in the cabinet. Before accepting Mrs Thatcher's offer, he made two conditions, both of which she fulfilled: membership of the 'E' Cabinet Sub-committee on Economic Affairs (chaired as one would expect by Mrs Thatcher), and more money for Wales from the Treasury. Walker is a traditional 'One Nation' Tory, an advocate of 'caring capitalism'. He was determined that South Wales in particular should share the prosperity of Southern England, and public funds were siphoned into Wales along the M4 and the line of the old Great Western Railway. Wales, with 5 per cent of the population, has, since 1987, received 20 per cent of Britain's inward investment, and is now known to the saloon bar boyos as 'little Japan beyond England'.

In the past, the Tories in Wales were the 'English' party, as disestablished as the Church. The Liberals were the conservatives, Labour the radical party, its power based on the pits. The Nats were a handful of bards and bombers. Today, the Tory party can claim to speak for the Principality. A 5 per cent swing to the Conservatives at the 1991 general election would give the Tories the largest number of seats in Wales, but not the largest number of votes, as the Labour party piles up huge majorities in its mining seats. Such a contribution would be very welcome to the Tory party in search of a fourth general election victory. It might have transformed Peter Walker's chances of succeeding Mrs Thatcher when the time eventually comes for her to step down. There are several old political saws. 'If you are in a hole, stop digging' is one. 'Never apologise, never explain' is another. 'Never resign' is yet another. Walker, who never bothered to disguise his hostility to much that Mrs Thatcher has done, seemed too competent a minister, and too shrewd a political operator to be easily got rid of. Did he not get the better of Arthur Scargill, his tactical sense complementing Mrs Thatcher's iron will?

Julian Amery is a different sort of 'pro'. He has been pickled in aspic. The son of Leo Amery who was of Levantine origin, Amery inhabits a time-warp of his very own. He is still a man of the 'thirties: sleek, lapel-grasping, plummy and patriotic. Youngish Tory MPs might be excused were they to believe him to be a former Foreign Secretary, so portentous are his pronouncements on foreign affairs. Sir Alec Douglas Home is said to have kept him away from the Foreign Office on the grounds that 'Julian would be always declaring war.' He is the very last Tory MP to have had a good war, spending much of it behind the enemy's lines in Albania. He lives rather grandly in a large flat in Eaton

Square, and is often to be found in the bar of White's. He is married to a daughter of Harold Macmillan's, and now sits securely for a Brighton seat, having once represented Preston in Lancashire. No Andaman islander has ever caught so strange a political fish. Like the coelacanth he is a survivor; to hear him address the House (he does not 'speak') is to return to the pages of Harold Nicolson and 'Chips' Channon. Between him and Mr Terry Dicks, a great gulf is fixed.

Terry Dicks is the most right-wing Conservative MP. He is no Imperialist, as is Amery. Dicks is what Andy Roth has described as 'a back street Conservative', a populist of a sort that would bring a blush to Mrs Thatcher's cheek. Dicks suffers from cerebral palsy. His stone age views can be catching. Who can fail to admire an MP who dislikes opera (and its subsidy) and who has described it as 'an overweight Italian singing in his own language'; the ballet as 'a man prancing about in a pair of ladies' tights'; and Bernie Grant's Queen's Speech outfit as 'looking like a Nigerian washerwoman'? In private life he is an engaging fellow: in public he scares the pants off any Tory to the left of John Carlisle. Yet he fulfils a purpose: he says the things other Tories would take care not to, thereby absolving many of us from making ritual obeisance in the direction of our natural supporters.

I suppose the real test of an MP's reputation is whether or not his colleagues stay put in their places when he rises to speak; or, come hurrying in from shire and suburb once his name flashes up on the monitor screens which fill the Palace. Circumstances can alter cases. Had Mrs Currie spoken immediately after her resignation, even I might have been seduced away from the *à la carte*. But such would be an extraordinary event. The litmus test is the routine performance, and there are very few who would pass it on both counts. Sir Peter Tapsell in an adversely critical mood about the Government's economic policies: Mr Michael Foot in defence of Neil Kinnock's party leadership: Mr Tam Dalyell with new evidence of wrongdoing on the part of the great at the time of Westland. Even so, it is hard to think of anyone who is so polished and predictable a performer as to make his friends and enemies come running. Perhaps the whips have creamed off the talent, placing it in positions of obscurity in junior office, leaving the backbenches to the undistinguished. I would go into the Chamber to listen to John Biffen who is never dull and often witty; to Michael Heseltine because as his biographer I have a vested interest in observing his performances, and to Denis Healey if he has the Prime Minister between his sights. They are the swans in a confederacy of ducks.

Mind you some of us ducks are gaily coloured. Mr Robert Rhodes James is the country's most distinguished biographer. A former Clerk of the House, he retails a fine line in pessimism. He is a frequent winner of the 'It is being so cheerful as keeps me going, despite the vicissitudes of public life' Award. Miserable he may sometimes be, but it is curious that someone so intelligent has never been given a chance to shine on the Conservative front bench. Mr Merlyn Rees, the former Labour Home Secretary, has achieved parliamentary 'sainthood'. This Merlyn's magic does not always lie in his clarity of expression. In the dear, dead days when Merlyn Rees faced Willie Whitelaw across the floor of the House, there was a competition in verbal obscurity, although Willie never went as far as to accuse his shadow of 'going round the country stirring up apathy'. Nor did he employ that other famous Willieism: 'we must not pre-judge the past'. Merlyn Rees is a dealer in decency; his views are always moderately expressed, nicely judged and eminently reasonable.

What should we make of women MPs? I suppose they have never been the same since Lady Astor. I do not count Mrs Thatcher as one. She transcends sex. At the height of the eggs and cheese row in February 1989, she was warned jokingly by Lord Young at a Downing Street Monday morning lunch not to take a portion of unpasteurised camembert. The Prime Minister angrily struck the table with the handle of her knife: 'I am not old or pregnant,' she cried. Frankly, I doubt if David Young or anyone else had any doubt on either score.

Mrs Barbara Castle was as feminine as she was formidable. As a young woman, her flaming red hair, to say nothing of her political views, set many a Tory heart afire. In those days we practised the politics of consensus. Mrs Virginia Bottomley is today's forces' sweetheart. Half the Tory party is secretly in love with her: Edwina Currie hopes that the other half is in love with her. Tall, handsome and charming, Virginia is the one junior minister whose books I would gladly carry. But my days as a parliamentary private secretary are sadly over. She is not only moderate of view, but clever and pretty with it, a rare combination in today's Tory party. There was for a time speculation to the effect that she was to be invited to become the first woman Tory whip, but it was not to be. Our whips refused to moderate their language. Instead she was sent to the Department of the Environment as a junior minister with the brief to turn Nicholas Ridley into a human being. She will rise effortlessly into the cabinet, although after Mrs Thatcher's sixty glorious years it will be some time before the Tory party picks another woman as leader. Peter and Virginia Bottomley are representatives of what might be called the high minded upper middle class such as the Huxleys or the Butlers. They are Tories with a social conscience, properly concerned with the welfare of the less fortunate, believers in 'One Nation' Toryism. They sit somewhat uncomfortably in a party which has been given over in recent years to arrivistes and garagistes. Living as I do in Farnham in her constituency I can vouch for her effectiveness as an MP; the local papers devote many columns to her activities, not least to the time she roller-skated along West Street to the applause of the burghers of Farnham. Her parliamentary neighbours did look askance at such Diana-like behaviour. I cannot easily imagine Mr Cranley Onslow, the stately chairman of the '22, entertaining the electors of Woking in the same way. But then he is obliged to skate on even thinner ice.

Tory men become knights, although their virtues are not always Arthurian. Tory women became Dames, although few of them can sing as well as Ethel Merman. Dame Janet Fookes could become the first woman Speaker. She is a most successful chairman of committees, a passionate animal lover and the possessor of a keenly-developed sense of fun. She can sometimes be seen dining with Mr Charles Irving, the Tory MP for Cheltenham and the Chairman of the Kitchen Committee of the Commons.

It would be fun to think that she cooks for hungry MPs while he waits at table, but that would be going too far. Charles Irving, who is known to the younger MPs as 'Mr Charles', owing to his habit of standing by the restaurant door wringing his hands in greeting, has not yet been knighted. He has done wonders with our food and deserves recognition.

It is often said that Conservative party constituency selection committees are prejudiced against women candidates. Few certainly are chosen. An ambitious woman in our party, it appears, has either to be twice as good (la belle Virginia) or twice as lucky. The truth is that far fewer women put themselves forward, and those that do run the risk of falling foul of their prejudiced sisters. 'Kinder, Kirche, Küche' is still the motto of many Conservative activists. Yet once they arrive at Westminster their chances of promotion are marginally better than those of the men. There is always room for several statutory women in Government while the really able ones, like Angela Rumbold or Sally Oppenheim-Barnes, can make their own way upwards.

Who is likely to succeed Mrs Thatcher when the time comes for her to go to Dulwich? The question is often posed, although there are colleagues who consider it to be faintly in bad taste. Such hesitations do them credit but they are easily soluble in the House claret. I have touched on Peter Walker, once Margaret's proconsul in Wales. He must be considered an outsider. His support is confined to the left of the party, and he would find it hard to broaden appreciably his appeal. His mirror-image must be Norman Tebbit, whose courage has made him friends, his tongue enemies. Norman is the best body puncher in politics, but he has tended to offend his friends almost as much as he has done his foes. He has disclaimed the Peacock Throne, satisfying himself with the self-appointed post of 'keeper of the sacred flame'. Norman is too right-wing even in today's party to be *papabile*.

Were Mrs Thatcher to fall under a bus, Sir Geoffrey Howe could take her place in the sun. So vivid a contrast in style and substance would be welcome to many, although I hasten to write that I do not favour so violent a transition. Howe is a lovely man who is only dull on his feet. In private he is as witty as he is wise. He is also courteous, patient and a good listener. He is a man of the respectable right whose 'radicalism' is of long standing. He was worrying about the future of welfare when still a young man, spending his salad days putting pen to pamphlet in the dingy offices of the Bow Group while his peers sang and danced the night away. His task as Foreign and Commonwealth Secretary was to travel the world dustpan and brush in hand, clearing up after the Prime Minister. A Howe Premiership would be restful. And he is good on television. He does not hector. Were I ever to be in a position to vote in a leadership election, I would as a moderate, first look elsewhere; were I not to find what I wanted, I would be happy to vote for Geoffrey Howe.

Edwina Currie has long courted publicity. She is a right-wing Conservative in tune with the temper of her times. She sprang to prominence when, at a party conference in the 'seventies, she brandished a pair of handcuffs from the rostrum (the debate was, predictably enough, on law and order) and threatened to chain herself to the podium until crime was a thing of the past. The newspapers loved her. A pretty woman, dark and vivacious, of the kind who would not wear a hat to a garden party, she was a natural: the rest of us, unwilling guests at this spectacle, feared the worst. 'We have a ripe one here,' was the comment of a party agent.

Her rise to fame and fortune has been uninterrupted. Every year my agent in Aldershot tells me whom the local party would wish me to invite as the guest at their annual dinner: Norman Tebbit, Jeffrey Archer and Edwina Currie; so far, I have resisted the temptation. To some Tories, Edwina is a pushy woman with too big a mouth, and hostility towards her is strongest among Northern Tory MPs who take offence at her strictures about North Country dietary habits. Mr Richard Holt has pursued her, if not to the grave then to, at least, perdition. Others, of a nicer nature, tend to shrug her off as a 'character' with whom they want no dealing, but whose uncrushability calls for admiration. She is clearly no fool. I took a delegation of constituents to see her on a local health matter, and she handled them with charm and skill. She is tenacious, plucky and totally self-absorbed. She has won the admiration of the Prime Minister, who, were she to live for ever, would no doubt attempt to smuggle her back into junior office. But to which department would she be sent? I can see cabinet ministers paling at the prospect of having Edwina in their team. She is neither Scottish nor Welsh. Northern Ireland is altogether too sensitive a posting. The Foreign and Common- wealth Office must be 'out', even after Mr David Mellor's stint; the Treasury might well look askance, Education would pull up the drawbridge. I can only suggest the Ministry of Labour where she could help Mr Michael Howard with the trade unions, passing round the sandwiches (low fat) and the beer (even lower gravity). Or, if not the Ministry of Labour, how about the Tory Whips' Office?

In January 1989, when the egg crisis was at its height, I was wakened by a knock at the door of my office under the roof of the Palace of Westminster. It was 5 o'clock in the afternoon, and I had been dozing in my regulation-issue arm chair. I have always felt that a siesta is one way of surviving the parliamentary day. I have a room of my own, a rare privilege for an MP, and the equivalent of a long service and good conduct medal. My caller was a secretary to the whip in charge of accommodation. 'We want you', she said, 'to share your room with Edwina Currie.'

It would be hard to imagine a ruder awakening. I murmured something to the effect that to do so would be like being at home all day, and then, gaining strength, listed my weaknesses: the odd cheap cigar, a taste for Burgundy, and a desire for privacy at any price. 'Oh you all say that,' sighed the girl and disappeared. It took some time to find a volunteer, but, eventually, Mrs Currie was closeted with Mr Greg Knight, the MP with whom she had once shared a room before becoming famous.

What should we make of la belle Edwina? I will not attempt to tell the story of the famous egg crisis, save to say that the original, off-the-cuff statement, delivered while trudging across some Derbyshire field, was exaggerated. It could, and should have been, swiftly corrected, 'much' being substituted for 'most'; had she done so, she might well have lived to go on telling the tale. The slip of her tongue was in character; those who live by the tabloids tend to die by them, but what is perhaps more interesting than Edwina herself has been the reaction to her as shown by her party colleagues. 'The most expensive woman since Helen of Troy' was among the more charitable.

Edwina Currie is the daughter of a Jewish tailor from Merseyside. Her friends say that she has been made the victim of male jealousy; her enemies that she had it coming. She probably has more enemies than friends. But when it comes to envy, her friends do have a point. Politicians can never make up their minds about publicity, they both crave and shun it. Ideally, we would like to control what it is the press write about us. The average MP is not particularly articulate; few of us write newspaper articles;

even fewer, books. Some of us make dull speeches, over-long, loyal and utterly predictable. Others hog the inside pages, standing ready at a moment's notice to come to the aid of a reporter in search of an instant comment, such as 'Harry Greenway blasts bishop'. The majority of MPS are content to see their names in local papers, and their occasional appearances on telly limited to regional programmes late at night. Such modesty is greatly to their credit; but what is even plainer is their suspicion of a handful of MPS, and ministers, who seem to get more than their fair shares of the plums – and the 'plums' are the sugared sort, sweetened by cheques.

I suppose I must plead guilty to being one of the 'media members'. I write for newspapers, appear on BBC's Radio 4 ('Out of Order') and have popped up at least once on all the major networked television programmes. In mitigation I would plead that political unemployment has obliged me to earn a living in the black economy. Had I been asked to be Parliamentary Secretary at the Ministry of Health, I like to think I would have been a touch more circumspect. Perhaps the best example of all is the Labour MP for Great Grimsby, Mr Austin Mitchell. He was sacked from his minor post on the Opposition front bench in January 1989 for taking Rupert Murdoch's shilling and appearing on Sky Television in the company of Mr Norman Tebbit. Austin has always been a freewheeler, a right-wing Labour MP, part don, part populist, whose remorseless sense of fun and irreverence ('Mrs Thatcher has flipped, Neil has flopped and David Steel flapped . . .') has not always endeared him to the grey-faced men who occupy the Labour Whips' Office. Mitchell is a sunny character who moves around the corridors of the Palace of Westminster like some great ship, escorted by a bevy of American girl researchers. The announcement (unconfirmed) that Mitchell was to receive £30,000 a year from Murdoch was enough to rally Labour behind Neil Kinnock despite the poor timing of his ultimatum to Mitchell.

Sir Clement Freud was another MP who was better known beyond Westminster than within it. Whenever he rose to his feet, looking remarkably like King Edward VII, he would be greeted by barks, a tribute to his highly-paid appearance on a dog food telly commercial. Freud is a funny man who has made a successful living from his wits. But he was curiously dull in the Commons. His duller colleagues could never understand the secret of this Liberal cook, whose style owed more to the Playboy Club, of which he was once a director, than to the halls of nonconformity. They loved him, for a time, in the Isle of Ely, but in the end even there his luck ran out. He lost his seat in 1987 and was given a handle to his name by Mr David Steel.

The 'media member' is not a new phenomenon. In my first incarnation Richard Crossman, Michael Foot, and Tom Driberg were among the best known political celebrities in the country. Desmond Donnelly and Woodrow Wyatt were the frequent guests of editors, and we should not forget Aidan Crawley. Media men were not so common on the Tory benches; having been elected both Chris Chataway and Geoffrey Johnson Smith kept off the box. The only television celebrity on our side was Stephen McAdden, the MP for Southend, and Charles Curran, an old-fashioned polemical journalist. Scribbling à la Boothby ('what a shit') was most certainly not the thing.

If I have descended over the years, Tony Benn has risen in place. He now sits high up on the Opposition backbench. In 1959, he was known as 'Anthony Wedgwood Benn', soon to become, as was the nature of things, Lord Stansgate. Today, he sits, his name truncated; his prospects nil. Were socialism a religion, Tony Benn would be a saint. In a previous incarnation a century back, he would have been an Anglican divine whose erratic progress to the gates of Rome and back would have been the cause of much comment. The Queen might well have disapproved of him. He would have entered the lists as a well loved clerical eccentric, a type which has long been England's pride and joy. In a yet more distant incarnation, in the year AD 989, he might have spent his life perched on the top of a pillar of rock. Benn's progress leftwards was encouraged by his time in Harold Wilson's cabinets, which must have been a corroding experience. It is perhaps unfair to try to make Tony into a figure of fun. Whatever his views may be (and no one can ever be absolutely certain of them), they have invariably been expressed with a fluent courtesy. Now that Sir Jasper More, the Tory MP for Ludlow, is dead, Tony Benn has the best manners of any Member of Parliament.

Jasper More retired from Parliament in 1983. He was almost the last of the library squires in the Tory party. Our knights generally rode hard to hounds, leaving their 'books' safe in the hands of estate managers. The Mores were South Shropshire gentry, living at Linley Hall near Bishop's Castle for five hundred years. My forebears touched their caps to the Mores: I was the first of my mother's family to be invited to spend the weekend at the great house. Jasper can be glimpsed in the 1960 portrait of the House, but, sadly, by the time of the Mendoza picture he had died. His courtesy was famous. When in 1986 I spoke in Ludlow at a Tory party dinner, his successor in the seat, Eric Cockeram, was absent in South Africa. On my plate was a letter of welcome – from Jasper More.

David Walder is another ghost. He was elected for High Peak at a by-election in 1961, too late for the Macmillan picture: he died of a heart attack in '78, far too soon for Miss Mendoza. Walder became a whip in Ted Heath's Government, but he was famous for his wit and irreverence. He wrote novels about love in the Young Conservatives – pretty suburban girls playing tennis in Gladstone Park. He was an historian who wrote about Nelson and the Graeco/Turkish war of the 1920s. He was a barrister to boot. Best of all, perhaps, was his capacity for friendship, his remorseless sense of the ridiculous and his capacity to live life, as the staider *Times* obituarists would put it, 'to the full'. I doubt if he would have prospered under Mrs Thatcher.

Sitting next to one another on the Government benches below the gangway are those two 'exiles from office', Michael Heseltine and Cecil Parkinson. Cecil, who has been unlucky in love, has the confident air of one who waits for an inevitable rehabilitation. He has a friend in high places. Michael seems to be gazing at a more distant horizon. He had just been plain unlucky. Cecil Parkinson is a kind of de luxe model of Sir Norman Fowler; the same horsepower but, unlike Norman, covered in a coat of metallic paint. He enjoys central locking and runs on white walled tyres. Michael Heseltine, on the other hand, seems to be seated as if to receive the attentions of a sculptor, who, having finished work on the white horse, is now ready to turn his attention to its rider.

Seated on the Government front bench is Mr Norman Tebbit, caught by the artist in the days before he fell out of friendship with Mrs Thatcher. Norman is the 'voice' of working class Conservatism. His courage after the atrocity at Brighton is much admired. Gaunt in appearance, mordant of tongue, he took politics by surprise after the '87 election when he forsook office in favour of the City of London. He keeps his candidature alive by many a nod and a wink, although, more modestly, he is on the record as having said that he will scrutinise Mrs Thatcher's putative successors for the rigour of their views. I reviewed his autobiography *Upwardly Mobile* for a Sunday paper. It is rancorous, but his early life is interesting – he literally took to the skies in order to escape an unhappy home, and his description of the Brighton bombing is most moving. He has promised to write a sequel to be entitled *The Sky's the Limit* in which Cecil Parkinson finally gets his girl and lives happily ever after.

As I have said, Tebbit is the best body puncher in politics. He cannot see a belt without hitting below it. He sits for Chingford on the Marches of Essex. Essex has become the home of the New Tory, the sons and daughters of London's East End who have moved away from the Hams and Canning Town in order to colonise the Essex Marches and to work for Ford's at Dagenham. Their aged parents have been left in the care of the East End Councils, dockers such as Alf Garnett, and their widows who are fearful of going out alone at night. The old East End has become black. The Marches are white; even the newsagents are white. As they moved eastwards into Essex so the sons of Alf Garnett moved away from the Labour party and embraced with all the passion of the convert, Mrs Thatcher's (and Tebbit's) brand of Conservatism. If you want to see what the Conservative party may become in twenty years go east to Billericay, as intellectuals in the 'twenties once went to Moscow. 'I have seen the future and it works.'

In Mendoza's picture Denis Healey is sitting next to Neil Kinnock. The party's leader is leaning forward, poised to submerge the Prime Minister under a torrent of wet, Welsh words. Healey seems pensive, as well he might be. The best leader Labour never had, Denis was defeated by Michael Foot in large part because of the defection of many right-wing Labour MPs to the Social Democrats. He was later a spectator when Kinnock beat Roy Hattersley for the leadership in 1983. I am happy to say

I have never been obliged to cross swords with Healey; although in the early 'sixties I once went on television with him to argue the toss. I remember waiting patiently for Denis to stop talking so that I might say my piece. He never did. Healey is the master of the parliamentary insult. Geoffrey Howe will long be associated with dead sheep. Mrs Thatcher has been called the Catherine the Great of Finchley and Florence Nightingale with a blow-torch. The funniest passage in a Healey front bench speech was the one in which he compared the members of Mrs Thatcher's cabinet (Margaret having gone reluctantly to Dulwich) with the prisoners in *Fidelio*.

Healey's high intelligence and higher horsepower made him into the most formidable Secretary of State for Defence, able to argue on equal terms with the defence intellectuals such as Thomas Schelling and Herman Kahn. As Chancellor he was the first to introduce monetary restraint, a policy which did little for his popularity among his party. Healey belongs to the most prestigious political club of all, that of people too good to be Prime Minister. His fellow members include Quintin Hailsham and Roy Jenkins.

In the Mendoza I can pick out two of the most promising Tories: Chris Patten and William Waldegrave. Patten, who was long suspected of holding Jacobite views, was first made to do time at the Foreign and Commonwealth Office, his task to dispense aid to the Third World. By so doing he won the approval of Sir Bob Geldof. Later Mrs Thatcher made him Secretary of State for the Environment in place of Nicholas Ridley. As a mark of her favour, the Prime Minister gave him the poll tax to sell to a far from grateful nation. Alderman Roberts must have paid his income tax in sorrow and his rates in anger; in consequence, Chris Patten has been responsible for making the working class pay for local government. I hope his reputation will not suffer unduly . . .

William Waldegrave has issued a statement saying that we have all been guilty of mispronouncing his name. I am still not certain what it is he wants us to call him. William has written a book called *The Binding of Leviathan* which is so densely argued that no other Tory, not even Sir Ian Gilmour, has been able to finish it. Today he is at the Foreign Office in place of Mr David Mellor.

When the two pictures are compared, the Mendoza is by far the

117

more colourful. In 1960 the Tory party was dressed in black. Thirty years later we are as gay as the Labour party was under Hugh Gaitskell. I am not convinced that we are politically more colourful. Skinner has not got Silverman's brains. Tony Beaumont-Dark, without whom no edition of 'The World at One' is complete, is in the Midlands tradition of Sir Gerald Nabarro, but a carbon copy nonetheless. Geoffrey Dickens, the 20 stone ex-amateur boxer, is a natural: his views may be frightful but in person he bears out Belloc's dictum that most people are much nicer than you first feared. I am not certain if that would apply to Mr Nigel West, or is it Rupert Allason? The Left is today less well represented. In the early 'sixties its ranks included Dick Crossman, Tom Driberg, and Michael Foot. Only Tony Banks promises as well, although were Ken Livingstone to call off his boycott of the Palace of Varieties, he, too, could be a contender. In the 'sixties Reggie Paget sat on the Labour benches and rode to hounds; today he sits in the Lords.

Life in Parliament is pleasing. Politics can explode suddenly as over the Falklands, or Profumo. When it does so the Chamber becomes a theatre, a cockpit in which the champions are pitted the one against the other, and reputations can be lost, or won, upon a single speech. It is always unwise to write off colleagues or opponents as being hopelessly dull, idle or unpromising. There are late developers even in the House of Commons. What will surprise strangers is the lack of personal animosity. Bad temper is generally left behind in the Chamber. What hatreds there are flourish within the parties where competition is keen, and ideology important. But 'hatred' is far too strong a word. We have all got our lists of people who we think are boring or unpleasant, and with 372 Tories to choose from, to say nothing of the other side, it is easy to avoid the unspeakable. It is unusual for Tory 'wets' to dislike Conservative 'dries', although temperatures can rise in the late autumn when the Tory party holds its annual elections for office to the backbench committees. It is at such times that Mr Gerald Gardiner, the lugubrious whipper-in for the loyal Thatcherites, can be glimpsed in corridors pressing the flesh. We 'wets' have our organisers: Mr Peter Temple-Morris who as MP for Leominster is the heir to the Mortimers, and the gallant Colonel Michael Mates whose amiable prejudices belie his belligerent appearance.

118

What has changed is the flavour of the regime. Under Harold Macmillan we were ruled by pragmatists who made no virtue out of doctrine, and who preferred style to substance. The backbenches were the home either of the loyal and unheeding or of the disaffected right, who looked backwards beyond Churchill to Chamberlain. Today, Maggie Rules, OK?, and the party's moderates recruit their strength for the eventual War of the Succession. The backbenches look eastwards towards the Marches of Essex. Mrs Thatcher's long period of rule may yet come to be regarded as a golden age; anything can happen. Last year we 'wets', mindful that 1989 saw the tenth anniversary of Mrs Thatcher's coming to power, greeted each other surreptitiously with the cry 'only 990 more years'.

# 9

# *The Rise and Rise (and Fall?) of Mrs Thatcher*

WHO COULD be neutral about Mrs Thatcher, her policies and her personality? She is either loved or hated, flattered or abused. When people talk of disliking politicians ('I can't bear Kinnock . . .'), what they usually mean is that they disapprove of his or her policies or attitudes. Few people can claim acquaintance with the leading political figures of the day; even backbenchers remain very largely spectators of events. A dominant two-party system forces people to make choices between the rival spokesmen, and it is always easier to love your own side and hate the other. An exception to this rule was, at one time at least, the attitude of many Conservatively inclined members of the middle classes when confronted with Dr David Owen. He did seem to talk sense, and to look good while doing so. What we generally do is to project our animosities upon our foes and our sympathies upon our friends. When it came to art, Alderman Foodbotham of Bradford 'knew what he liked': when it comes to politics, partisans, and they are the ones who matter, have little time for equivocation.

Politicians are supposed to be partisan. Not since the war has there been an Independent elected to the House of Commons. The Lords are permitted the luxury of doubt, and there are crossbenches provided for those who refuse to align themselves with one set of attitudes or another. The Commons however is a confrontational chamber, and Mrs Thatcher is a self-

121

acknowledged 'conviction politician'. Indeed, when challenged she has drawn the parallel of the Apostles themselves; 'Do you think you would ever have heard of Christianity if the Apostles had gone out and said "I believe in consensus"?' she asked an American journalist. It is this sense of conviction which explains much of her success, and tells one more about the sort of public person she is. Conviction politics is all very well, but it does tend to mean a lack of respect for the convictions of others, and its practice can lead one swiftly into the paths of self-righteousness. I think Mrs Thatcher is an unattractive public person; she grates on television; what she is like as a private individual I cannot really say. I have only spoken to her on four occasions in twenty-five years at Westminster.

If I recount the four occasions on which we met it will be to illustrate the isolation of the political foot soldier. Aldershot Tories probably believe that she and I meet on a regular basis; her encouragement being matched by my admiration. The electorate, if it thinks about the matter at all, no doubt believes front and back benches to live inside each others' pockets. We do not. Prime Ministers arrive in the Commons' chamber on Tuesday and Thursday afternoons at 3.13 p.m. precisely. They answer questions for fifteen minutes and then disappear behind the Speaker's chair, bound either for their suite of rooms 'behind the chair' or for Downing Street. A Prime Ministerial speech is an annual event which can take place if a motion of no confidence is tabled by the Opposition. A Prime Ministerial visit to the tea room can be taken as a sign of political anxiety. I sat and watched one such visit recently. Mrs Thatcher was escorted by her parliamentary private secretary, Mark Lennox-Boyd. Three other Tories were at table, tea to hand but rock cakes forgotten. An intense Mrs Thatcher talked to them; they sat with such expressions on their faces as if they were undergoing a religious experience. Lennox-Boyd seemed less enraptured, but then he had doubtless heard it all before.

My first encounter with Mrs Thatcher was at lunch in the early 'sixties. She joined a table together with Peter Kirk and David Walder. After she had left David Walder exclaimed, 'My God, she is like the chairman of my women's committee in High Peak – but writ hideously large'. Margaret's fundamentalism was, at that time, deeply unfashionable. But she has had the last laugh. In the late 'seventies, when the party was in opposition, I was approached by her private office to help her with a speech she had been invited to give to the annual dinner of the Institute of Journalists. I was at the time chairman of the party's Media Committee and was helping Willie Whitelaw on the front bench on broadcasting matters. I wrote a speech for her and included several jokes with which she might put her audience at its ease. I learnt later that the jokes had misfired, having been told badly. The laughs did not come. In retrospect, I blame myself. Women are no good at telling jokes in public, and Mrs Thatcher is no Maureen Lipman. At any road I was not asked to put pen to paper on her behalf again.

The next occasion on which we met must have been in 1981, when, as a vice-chairman of the party's Defence Committee, I accompanied the officers who were invited on an annual basis to attend upon the Prime Minister in Downing Street. This meant a pilgrimage up Whitehall led by a nervous Sir Anthony Buck, the chairman, whom we primed as to the points he should raise on our behalf. John Nott, the Secretary of State for Defence, was planning to 'sink' the Royal Navy as part of his defence cuts, and the party, or a good slice of it, was up in arms.

We were ushered into an ante-chamber in Downing Street where the flock wallpaper had something in common with an Indian restaurant. All that seemed lacking was a blow-up coloured photograph of the Himalayas. After a short wait we were invited into the drawing room. Tony Buck said little and the Prime Minister said much. Winston Churchill ('young Winston') attempted an anecdote about his grandfather, while I admired the mantelshelf on which were placed several handsome Victorian Staffordshire figures of Cobden, Wellington and the like. 'Julian,' said the Prime Minister severely, 'why are you looking around the room?' I admitted to admiring the furniture. We left with most of our ammunition unexpended. Happily the cuts in naval strength had not taken place before the Argentinians invaded the Falkland Islands.

In the early 'eighties I was sitting at lunch in the Members' Dining Room when I caught sight of Ian Gow who was then her PPS. A jovial disconcerting man, Gow was the harbinger of ill fortune. His task was to case the joint; to make certain that the Prime Minister could be seated among friends. She entered, sat down, ordered a poached egg on Bovril toast, and filled the silence which had fallen on the company with a series of pointed interrogations. 'Tell me, Julian, what are your views on the money supply?' For a second or two I might have been a cabinet minister. The ordeal did nothing for my digestion; what was worse was the effect she had on the table at large. Everyone began to outdo his neighbour in sycophancy. Twenty years ago I had experienced a similar visitation when Harold Macmillan joined my table. He had listened and he had made us laugh.

The fourth occasion was in the late 'eighties when the survivors of the 1959 intake, which, incidentally, had been once described by Rab Butler as 'the worst in his experience', met in Dining Room B to celebrate their longevity. Fifteen or so survivors of the Macmillan election when the Tories had been returned to power with a majority of 100, enjoyed a jolly dinner and two speeches: one by Mrs Thatcher, clearly the most distinguished 'fifty-niner' of us all, and the other by me. My part in the proceedings had been suggested by Sir William Clark, whose utter loyalty to Margaret and her economics had been mirrored twenty years ago by Brigadier Jacky Smythe's devotion to Harold Macmillan. I made what I hoped was a tactful, yet funny speech which amused, and did not offend, all save the subject of it. (Sir Peter Tapsell, who was a fellow diner, told the whips afterwards that it had been brilliant. I boast only to put the event into a proper context.)

Mrs Thatcher responded in characteristic style. She said little and smiled not at all. When she had finished and we were on our feet, Bill Clark grabbed Margaret and me by our elbows and told us to bury the hatchet. In consequence, the Prime Minister and I walked solemnly from the restaurant floor to the Members' Lobby along the corridor from the Library which, at that time in the evening, was lined by lobby correspondents. Mouths dropped open and a hush fell as we walked the length of the corridor seemingly deep in conversation. In fact, Mrs Thatcher said only one thing that I can remember. 'The party', she said, 'had gone too far to the left before I took over.'

Those who would understand Margaret Thatcher should travel

to Grantham. The corner shop, once owned by her formidable father Alderman Alfred Roberts, is now a run-of-the-mill restaurant named the Premier. It stands on what was once the Great North Road, up and down which lorries must have thundered between London and the industrial North. The building is today part restaurant, part shrine, for the original 'thirties shop has been recreated and the hungry are obliged to pass through it in order to eat. There are shelves of jams which bear the Roberts label, the very counter behind which the young Margaret learnt the rudiments of national housekeeping, and a set of scales. Sacks of flour and sugar line the walls and the calendars are suitably admonitory.

The Roberts were Methodists, hard-working Lincolnshire people of the kind whose ancestors would have marched with Cromwell. They must have hovered between the ranks of the respectable working class and the lower middle. Margaret's mother was by every account a simple woman. Mrs Thatcher is on record as having said that after the age of 15, she and her mother had nothing left to say to one another. There was a sister who is married to a farmer and who remains totally unknown to the public. Mrs Thatcher's father was the formative and dominant influence upon her life. Alfred Roberts was a Liberal.

Grantham has voted itself the most boring town in England, and one can see why. A handsome church, a scattering of Georgian town houses and a long main street, the town lies among the flat lands of Lincolnshire, transfixed not only by the Great North Road but by the main east coast route of the London and North Eastern Railway. Its most famous son is Isaac Newton, who was as cantankerous as he was brilliant. But Lincolnshire folk lack the Southern graces and even Northern warmth. Could it be the effect of the prevailing cold East wind? There are statues of Newton and a portrait of Alderman Roberts in the Town Hall, but no sign, save for the Premier restaurant, of Mrs Thatcher herself. No sign that is save for a mug which I discovered in a cheap shop on the way to the railway station. It carried a transfer of a small girl under which was the name 'Margaret Roberts' together with the caption 'I am a proper little Madame.'

Mrs Thatcher is an intuitive politician. She has articulated with great political success the views of the hitherto unfashionable lower middle class. She is a product of the 'Victorian virtues' which she defines as thrift, hard-work and not minding one's own business. How could she believe in minding one's own business? Mrs Thatcher is a moralist, one of nature's nannies. Grantham may have made her but she did not tarry long in the town. She escaped by scholarship to Oxford. Unlike Ted Heath whose relatively humble background she shares, she made no attempt to join the Establishment. When she was first elected to Parliament as MP for Finchley in 1959, her views were commonplace for a Conservative, if totally unfashionable. What we did not know, and could not tell until it was too late, was the extent of her indomitable will, her thirst for work, her unswerving sense of purpose. She was a roundhead in a party of royalists.

Margaret Thatcher's election as Tory party leader in 1975, which I have called elsewhere 'the Peasants' Revolt', proved various things about the Conservative party – including Sir John Hoskyns's dictum that the Tory party only panics in times of crisis. What Mrs Thatcher's election did not demonstrate, however, was the taking of a conscious decision to set out on the road to 'Thatcherism'. There was no such thing: even 'monetarism', later to become the touchstone of her counter-revolution, was an arcane technical expression, recognised only by a small group of backbenchers such as Nicholas Ridley and John Nott, who had maintained a running battle against the big-spending policies of Edward Heath's Government from 1972 to 1974. Having been brought down by the National Union of Miners in February 1974, and defeated the following October for the second time within a year, the morale of Conservative MPs had slumped to the level of 1945. We did not have to look far for the scapegoat.

The band of dissidents was swiftly reinforced. The newcomers were in no sense monetarists. Their doubts were about the leadership of the party. It would not be unfair to Mrs Thatcher, at that time relatively unregarded, to say that her election owed far less to her merits, such as they were, than to the general unpopularity of the party's leader. Hostility was especially marked among Tory backbenchers, most of whom had not shared with their leader the exhilaration of Government.

Edward Heath was by then a three-time loser. The achievements of his period of office were few, the problems he faced intractable. Entry into Europe will come to be regarded as Ted's triumph, an act of government that will be seen as more enduring than the reconquest of the Falkland Islands or the selling off of the family silver. But at the time the Conservative party suffered from a kind of post-coital depression with regard to Europe; perhaps too much had been asked of us; it was too great a leap in the dark. As leader, Heath had enjoyed one famous victory, in 1970, but before that he had lost the election of '66 (it might have been wiser to have ditched Sir Alec Douglas-Home after that election and not before it; it would certainly have done something for his successor's reputation), and now he had lost two elections in the same year, as did Bonar Law in 1910. In the first of them the Conservatives had polled more votes than Labour but the vagaries of the electoral system and Jeremy Thorpe's failure to carry his Liberals into a coalition, brought Harold Wilson back to Downing Street at the head of a minority Government. On our side, during that strange twilight world between the February and October elections, many of us thought the only way to break through what appeared to be the electorate's disgust with all the parties seemed to be some sort of national coalition. Indeed, when eventually Ted went to the country in the autumn it was on a platform of 'a government of national unity'.

As ever, there were other Tories who thought that the trouble was that the Conservatives had not been Conservative enough. In this respect the right of the party mirrors the left of Labour. The true believers thought they had found a leader in Sir Keith Joseph ('the only boring Jew I have met' was Harold Macmillan's view of him). Joseph followed in the steps of St Paul. He now claimed to have only recently discovered the true faith, having set up in the spring of 1974 the Centre for Policy Studies to reassert the case for a market economy and for the rolling back of the frontiers of the State. Mrs Thatcher became his deputy at the Centre. It did not go unremarked that these two were reformed sinners; they had been two of the biggest of the big spenders in the Heath Government, he at Social Services and she at Education.

The setting up of the Centre for Policy Studies contributed in due course to the division of the Conservative party. In the short term it brought back into prominence many of the politically discredited who saw their opportunity and, in company with Mrs Thatcher, were soon to take it, but the division within the party was nothing like as clear-cut as it was to become in the early years of Mrs Thatcher's premiership. There was a wide range of gradation and interpretation of what was needed in the party, but the biggest consideration in replacing Ted Heath was personality rather than policy.

Among potential successors, Mrs Thatcher was far down the list. There was no favourite to succeed. At one point Sir Keith Joseph was front runner until a silly speech about genetics made his supporters doubt his judgement. He withdrew his hat from the ring, citing the inadequacy of his temperament. There was support, too, for Edward du Cann, the long-time chairman of the 1922 Committee (comprising every Tory MP while the party was in opposition), and one-time chairman of the party itself. Du Cann was an enemy of Heath's and an active figure in the City of London. But it soon became clear that his City *persona* was too controversial for many tastes. Denied the leadership, he remained prominent among the conspirators. The point was that there was simply a desire to get Heath out; this was underlined by the noteworthy role of Airey Neave, who became Mrs Thatcher's campaign manager and without whose organising skills she might never have made it. Airey Neave was not at first a Margaret man. He was a dissident in search of a horse that would run. At first he tried to promote du Cann and would have been willing to promote Joseph. Only after they both fell at fences did he offer to organise her campaign.

There were other complications. Some Tory MPs wanted to put off an election until some more obvious candidate emerged, such as Christopher Soames who was serving in Brussels as a Euro-Commissioner. Another complication was the so-called 'cowards' charter'. The rules for the election of a party leader (copies of which are still available in the Government Whips' Office in the event of someone wishing to mount a challenge against Mrs Thatcher) laid down that there would be two stages, and possible candidates could reserve their position for the second round. This was designed for the convenience of Heath's closest colleagues, like Willie Whitelaw, James Prior, Robert Carr and Sir Geoffrey Howe, who were not prepared to stand against their chief, but would put themselves forward in the event of Heath failing to survive the first round. It was this scrupulousness which cost Whitelaw the leadership of the Tory party.

It meant that someone had to bell the cat by standing in the first round. Mrs Thatcher made the most of her opportunity. She was not expected to win, but, in fact, and largely thanks to the unremitting efforts of Airey Neave, she won more votes than Ted Heath in a three-cornered contest, the third man being the eccentric Hugh Fraser. Humiliated, Heath withdrew to the undisguised glee of his enemies. At this the other candidates, the Heath men, duly presented themselves for the second round. They could reasonably expect that one or the other of them would receive a large proportion of Mrs Thatcher's first round 'protest' votes, but politics does not work like that. Fortune favours the brave, and Mrs Thatcher went on to win the second round too.

The arena in which the election took place was Committee Room 14, the only committee room large enough to accommodate the '22 or the parliamentary Labour party. The '22 meets once a week in 'peacetime'; in times of crisis it can become a theatre both of cruelty and of the absurd, offering an element of drama which the Commons' chamber seems reluctant to provide. The run-of-the-mill weekly meeting is to be avoided. A whip reads out the business of the coming week, the minutes of the last meeting are recited, there may be a listless question or two from a predictable source and that is that. What humour there is can only be of the unconscious kind. But when the party's dander is up, the '22 can be every bit as Gothic as its High Victorian surroundings. I can remember three such occasions: Mrs Thatcher's defeat of Ted Heath, the trial of Lord Carrington after the invasion of the Falklands; and the revenge taken on Leon Brittan at the height of the Westland affair. And there was a fourth: the ordeal of Alasdair Milne and John Howard of the BBC at the time of the Falklands War. It is on occasions such as these that the worst side of Our Great Party manifests itself. Unleashed, we run the gamut of our emotions: jingoism, anti-semitism, obscurantism, cant and self-righteousness; all play their part. We can, when pushed to do so, flourish our political prejudices like so many captive princes paraded through the streets of Imperial Rome.

129

Why not hold such meetings in the Coliseum? And charge an admission fee? In which case we would have no need to reward generous industrialists with knighthoods.

Mrs Thatcher's elevation to the Peacock Throne was hailed by the minority of monetarists, and by sundry other political comentators whom nobody had ever thought of as being particularly Conservative; people like the one-time editor of the *New Statesman*, Paul Johnson, who sensed that in Mrs Thatcher they might have at last a politician who could overturn the traditionalists of the Conservative party more effectively than the socialists had ever been able to do. Much of her most zealous support did come from people outside the Tory party, for example Alfred Sherman, a former Marxist who had turned towards Manchester. But the zealots had only one of her ears. Mrs Thatcher combines caution with conviction. She kept Ted Heath's shadow cabinet more or less intact. She even resurrected a former Chancellor who had never shown the least instinct for monetary restraint, Reginald Maudling, and appointed him 'shadow' foreign secretary. Reggie was later to be sacked, a sick and disappointed man. He had tried, so he explained to me one lunchtime, to soften Mrs Thatcher's fiercely anti-Soviet views, but 'the woman was impossible'.

If she was truly impossible, it took 'the colleagues' some time to find out. Her speeches in the country took on a forthright tone, even if several of her performances from the Opposition front bench in the House were remarkably poor. She is no orator. Her style is to read from a brief, lovingly prepared by relays of her helpers. In the Commons she tends to lecture, to read rapidly from her script, volume providing what emphasis she believes to be necessary. She tends, too, to place the emphasis on the wrong word. Practice has made her proficient at conference oratory where she was one of the first to make use of the magic mirrors which enabled President Reagan to win for himself the reputation of being the 'great communicator'. Her message is invariably upbeat although when she does not exhort she scolds. She is an uncomfortable performer. If it were not for the fact of the office she holds she would be unlistenable to.

The agenda for Government did not rest wholly in the hands of the shadow cabinet. Between her election as party leader and the general election of May 1979 which brought her to power, she built up her own team of advisers, many of them based on the Centre for Policy Studies (CPS) which now emerged as co-existing in friendly, and often downright unfriendly, rivalry with the Conservative Research Department. It was through the CPS that Mrs Thatcher recruited men like John Hoskyns and David Young, businessmen, not politicians, who later came to have more power than cabinet ministers. Jim Prior has written in his memoirs, *A Balance of Power*, how astonished he was when he found, once the party was in office, that Mrs Thatcher and her coterie were determined to translate their rhetoric into action: 'It was really an enormous shock to me that the budget which Geoffrey [Howe] produced the month after the election of 1979 was so extreme. It was then that I realised that Margaret, Geoffrey and Keith [Joseph] really had got the bit between their teeth and were not going to pay attention to the rest of us at all if they could possibly help it.'

He might have been less surprised had he been privy to what had been said by many into Mrs Thatcher's other ear. Even in Opposition the pattern which was later to become clear in Government was set. Small groups of sympathisers were already in place, groups which complemented the more formal shadow cabinet and cabinet apparatus. Is 'complemented' quite the right word? Viewed from the perspective of eleven years in Downing Street, opinions differ as to the reasons for so many *ad hoc* bodies which have played so large a part in her deliberations. Is their purpose to relieve the burden on a weekly cabinet meeting? Before Thatcher the cabinet used to meet twice a week. And thereby to facilitate business? Or have they been the means whereby the cabinet has been escorted in a particular direction favoured by the Prime Minister and her allies? Could the counter-revolution have taken place without them? I do not think so, but given the divisions of opinion within the party as to its direction, and the frequent disputes over the means to be employed, the Prime Minister cannot be blamed for fighting her corner. What her enemies failed to take into account was not so much her direction but the will with which she set about achieving her objectives. She has a will of iron.

Mrs Thatcher entered Downing Street with the words of St

Francis of Assisi (*via* Sir Ronald Miller) on her lips. They were to haunt her.

> Where there is discord, may we bring harmony,
> Where there is error, may we bring truth,
> Where there is doubt, may we bring faith,
> Where there is despair, may we bring hope.

Mrs Thatcher's apparent lack of a sense of humour in general, and her inability to laugh at herself, has been one of her greatest political strengths. She is totally immune to satire. She suffers abuse in plenty, frequently coming top in public opinion polls which seek to discover Britain's most irritating woman, but certainly appears to be armoured against such hostility. Her tactic at Prime Minister's Question Time is to lower her head and charge. The jibe she will return with interest: the joke goes unappreciated. She is quite incapable of using humour as a means of defusing a difficult situation. She seems to be without wit or humour. But she has many other qualities.

In the 'sixties, the so-called satirists of the BBC's 'That was the Week that Was' played a part in the downfall of Harold Macmillan and his Government. Sir Alec Douglas-Home, who was not the most sensible choice as his successor, suffered almost as much as Macmillan did from the attention of lampooners. Mrs Thatcher has been most savagely attacked by her detractors both of the left and the right but to no measurable effect. She is portrayed in 'Spitting Image' as a tyrant; as the only man in the cabinet. Her rubber traits include impatience, arrogance and vanity. Caricature can only go some way towards pinning the butterfly into the box, but the best and worst the satirists have attempted have not deflected her by one degree. This is because she is a crusader, and crusaders travel light, unburdened by doubts.

Harold Macmillan was a highly sensitive man who took the trouble to disguise his apprehension behind his Brigade tie. He knew what he wanted to achieve: decolonialisation and Britain's entry into Europe. Manchester Liberals (as opposed to the Hampstead kind) believed him to be a sentimentalist who had been corrupted by his time as MP for Stockton in the 'thirties when he had come to identify himself with the deserving poor. He suffered from bouts of depression – 'black dog' – and was acutely aware of the dangers of a third world war, the vulnerability of an economy to balance of payments crises, and the wariness with which he was regarded by the bulk of his backbenchers. To escape from his black dog, he read the novels of Jane Austen: to refresh himself he re-read the novels of Anthony Trollope. He once suggested that Mrs Thatcher would do well to go away and read a novel, but, sadly, he did not say which one. Mrs Thatcher was later to admit to having read Frederick Forsythe's *The Fourth Protocol* for the second time.

Mrs Thatcher's character is of a more robust kind. She is a stranger to introspection and does not seem to suffer from doubt. There is only one example of a lack of self-confidence: her remark at the height of the Westland affair that she might not be Prime Minister at the end of what threatened to be a most difficult day. She survived. In the ordinary course of events she is impossible to deflect. She is impervious to ridicule. Denis Healey has set out deliberately to make fun of her, and of her policies, in speeches from the Opposition front bench, performances which have given pleasure on all sides, but his victim remains untouched. Just as Oliver Cromwell was never deflected from his course ('God's will') by pot-house jokes, so Mrs Thatcher is unlikely to be made to falter in her course by Thames Television. She protects herself from adverse criticism by never reading the newspapers, only a digest carefully compiled by Mr Bernard Ingham. She does not watch television, although it is believed she listens every morning to the Radio 4 programme 'Today'. She has admitted to a taste for Larkin's exquisitely pessimistic poetry. Jeffrey Archer is the Court Novelist. Her self-confidence is buttressed by what she perceives to be the popularity of her populist views, and by the knowledge that the majority of her party's backbenchers live on her wave-length. 'Sticks and stones' must have been the motto of her father, Alderman Alfred Roberts.

# 10

# Divine Rule

W\ILL 'THATCHERISM' survive Mrs Thatcher? No other Prime
Minister has given birth to an 'ism' of his or her own. Nobody
speaks of Wilsonism, Heathism or Macmillanism: friend and foe
alike make free with the term 'Thatcherite'; to some, and not just
in the Labour, Liberal or Democrat parties, it is a convenient
term of abuse, to others a matter of pride. By affixing the label
'Thatcherite' to the politics of a decade, we have paid Margaret
Thatcher a huge compliment. Does she deserve it?

I am no 'Thatcherite' but I am forced to concede that she has
stamped her powerful personality on public life and set the
political agenda for the 'eighties and beyond. She has overcome
the opposition to her in the Tory party, an opposition which has
been obliged to go underground. She has treated her enemies
with a disdainful contempt, whether they are to be found sitting
next to her or behind her in the Commons, or across the floor of
the Chamber. She is as high-handed with foreigners, especially
European socialists, as she can be with her fellow countrymen.
Foreigners and children, many of whom cannot remember any
other occupant in Downing Street, have difficulty distinguishing
her from the Queen. She pops up at every national disaster, uses
the royal 'we', and regularly is voted 'Woman of the Year' by the
listeners to 'Today'. Can it be long before her head appears upon
our postage stamps?

But could we have Thatcherism without Thatcher? Such may
well be the slogan adopted by the contenders to the Tory
succession whenever she decides to call it a day. Dr John
Campbell, writing in the *Contemporary Review*, suggests that in
order to find the answer, her politics has to be divided into four

aspects: political philosophy in its broadest sense, the intellectual doctrine of monetarism with which she has been identified, the practical agenda of 'Thatcherism', and finally, the underlying instincts of Mrs Thatcher. It is as good a guide as any I have discovered.

The political philosophy which she holds, and holds very passionately indeed, embraces a concern for personal freedom under the law and the value of private property as a counter-weight to collectivism, and a general support for capitalism against socialism. Not every Conservative would feel quite as strongly as she does about all of them. But Mrs Thatcher feels strongly about everything.

Mrs Thatcher had never shown an interest in economics prior to 1975. Having won the leadership of the party, she found ready to hand a whole range of congenial ideas worked out by various right-wing groups whom it suited her to encourage and who were, in turn, delighted to find so powerful a champion of their beliefs. Hayek, Friedman and Harris became the Freeman, Hardy and Willis of Mrs Thatcher's new Conservatism; a store house with its own madame, its goods the belief that unlimited economic benefit would flow from the untrammelled operation of the free market. She has appeared to follow much of the new right's prescription, notably a non-Keynesian economic policy. Unemployment was allowed to rise to unprecedented levels, reflation was delayed at least until the recession, which had been deepened by the effect of Geoffrey Howe's first two budgets, had done its useful worst. And besides, trade union immunities have been reduced, levels of direct taxation cut, council houses sold off to tenants, much of the public sector has been 'privatised', and much of economic activity has been deregulated. Taken together the package can be described as 'Thatcherite', although not every aspect, for example trade union reform, belongs solely to the three Thatcher governments. The reforms carried out under Heath were more radical.

And yet, whatever her agenda, she is not quite the ideologue she likes to pretend to be. Defence spending has until recently been protected from the cuts on public spending which so characterised her early years in office. The National Health Service, despite a generalised hostility towards the principle of a service 'free' at the point of use, has been 'safe in our hands', an assurance which has only been rendered credible by further injections of public money. Education vouchers have not yet been introduced, although student loans will be. Home owners are still in receipt of mortgage tax relief up to £30,000. More seriously, perhaps, *laissez-faire* has been accompanied by measures that have served to centralise power at the expense of the independence of local government. Mrs Thatcher boasts, even at Tory party conferences, of her 'radicalism'. She has got away with it. She has done so, in part, by an act of will; in part, because of the changing social composition of the Tory party (as Mrs Thatcher has gone up in the world, so the Conservative party has gone down); and in part, because of the *Führerprinzip* which comes naturally to Tories, and which she has so generously fostered. Strongly patriotic though she is, there are today more of the party's blue banners in evidence in seaside halls than there are Union Jacks. It is tempting to use the word 'Nuremberg' to describe the atmosphere of adulation which now surrounds the leader's speech at the end of the annual party conference (and the poisonous hostility with which some of the younger Tories greet Ted Heath), but the comparison is not with Hitler, it is with Hugenberg. Mrs Thatcher is a nationalist, but no socialist, and no Nazi.

Of Dr Campbell's four strands, the last is the most interesting. What are her underlying political instincts? Here we can only return to Grantham. In the early days of her administration, I wrote that the country was being governed by the shade of Alderman Roberts, and we are still haunted by him even today. Mrs Thatcher is socially authoritarian. She is Nanny to the Nation, yet her values are shared by a large section of the British public. Her values include a robust nationalism which sees Jacques Delors, the chairman of the European Commission, as just as much an enemy as General Galtieri. She gives strong backing to the forces of law and order (so she should, given the remorseless rise in the crime rate), she is a believer in hanging, despite the opposition of home secretaries of the day, and she expresses a firm disapproval of sexual permissiveness, save, possibly, when practised by her cabinet ministers. Campbell describes these opinions as 'the social values of the hitherto politically neglected middle class'. They are the values of what I have called 'Billericay Man'.

It is difficult to steer a middle way between Mrs Thatcher's friends and foes. Professor Vincent, who is a journalist fit enough to do the splits, writing as he does both for Rupert Murdoch's *Sun* and *Times*, wrote in the *Contemporary Review* that hatred of her (which, in his view, comes from above rather than below the average income) is infected with snobbery. 'Mrs Thatcher is the point at which all the snobberies meet: intellectual snobbery, social snobbery, the snobbery of Brooks's, the snobbery about scientists of those educated in the arts, the snobbery of the metropolis about the provincial, the snobbery of the South about the North, and the snobbery of men about career women.' I can only murmur *touché*. Yet Vincent's admiration knows no bounds. He concludes his piece in this way: 'She has played a larger part in the nation's conversation than any Premier since Churchill. She has brought courage back into politics. And she did it without uncommon abilities, uncommon advantages, and despite the Tories.'

How can one possibly measure 'conversation'? And why 'since Churchill'? Did Clement Attlee go undiscussed? Or was Anthony Eden's attempt to overthrow Nasser at the time of Suez unremarked? Is Mrs Thatcher any more courageous than Ted Heath? So far, his conclusion owes more to the *Sun* than to *The Times*. But what of his last sentence? His three assertions as to her abilities, advantages, and the opposition of her own party, deserve further scrutiny.

Mrs Thatcher's abilities are in no way common. She is physically very strong indeed. Her capacity for sheer hard work is extraordinary. Her relish for politics seems undiminished even after her ten years in office. Her health is good. She can get by with four hours of sleep a night. She has an insatiable appetite for paper. She drinks relatively little, and eats less. She lacks subtlety and is without humour, but her focus, though narrow, is intense. She is very formidable. Just as Sir Keith Joseph claimed that as a Jew he was obliged to fire on all six cylinders, so, too, does Mrs Thatcher. Even those of us who feel uncomfortable with her, cannot deny a certain admiration. To claim, as Vincent does, that her abilities are nothing out of the ordinary is as good an example of the snobbery of the provincial don for the 'second-class Oxford chemist' (as Mrs Thatcher has been described by her tutor), as one might find in all Bristol.

What about her advantages? Was Mrs Thatcher as underprivileged as Vincent suggests? Life in the corner shop at Grantham may have been simple enough, but it was secure. Her childhood was in no way an unhappy one. The local girls' grammar school took the young Margaret to Somerville College, Oxford, on a scholarship. She got a Second in chemistry, became President of the Oxford Tories (the first woman to do so) and later became a barrister specialising in tax affairs. She married a rich man and has been, as far as one can tell, free of money worries since her mid-twenties. Has she been 'without uncommon advantages'? The truth is that she climbed whatever ladder was available with dexterity and has lived a charmed life. Many would envy her her advantages.

Vincent is on firmer ground when he asserts that she has succeeded 'despite the Tories'. What I think he means is that she has been able to overcome the opposition to her of many, but by no means every, Tory, since she first took office in 1979. She has used every weapon at her disposal to get her way. She has bullied and she has cajoled. She has sacked her enemies and promoted her friends. She has enjoyed the benefits of good fortune, and she has lived very dangerously indeed. Her behaviour over the Westland and *Spycatcher* affairs demonstrated a degree of arrogance, high-handedness and equivocation unmatched in recent British politics. And yet she has survived. What has been the secret of her success?

The answer lies in the ballot box. She has won three general elections. She has given the Tory party its heart's desire, office. She has been able to take advantage of her great good fortune – Galtieri's ambition, Scargill's bone-headedness, and the effect of the secession of the Gang of Four from the Labour party. She has done so for two reasons: she has enjoyed the support and affection of the bulk of the new Conservative party; and the inability of her opponents within the party to take advantage of her mistakes. She has held the centre of the ring and obliged her opponents to dance ineffectively around her.

After the 1981 budget which was harshly deflationary, the

so-called cabinet 'wets', Sir Ian Gilmour, Mark Carlisle and Peter Walker, among others, contemplated resignation. They agonised but decided to stay put – and were later sacked. Mrs Thatcher's first act upon her re-election in 1983 was to get rid of her foreign secretary, Francis Pym, with whom she had been on bad terms throughout the Falklands War. John Biffen, the Leader of the House, who had called in 1983 for a 'balanced ticket', was sacked the day after the Prime Minister's victory in 1987. Biffen told the world that 'he would not be in the business of making life easy for Mrs Thatcher'. Pym, on the other hand, went into the business of opposition. In 1985 he launched Conservative Centre Forward, a group thirty or so strong, pledged to keep the Tory party moderate. It failed to do so.

I was closely involved in the formation of Conservative Centre Forward. Francis Pym was the first of the 'wets' to translate his opposition to Mrs Thatcher, her style, and the content of much of her policy, into positive action. Gilmour had spoken out and had written much that was adversely critical of the New Order. Christopher Soames had spoken out in Pratt's and White's. Heath, it was popularly supposed, was sulking in his tent, although the former Prime Minister made many speeches that were hostile to aspects of Government policy in the House. Pym was the first to mount a public and organised challenge to the policies of his leader.

In the early months of '85, the 'conspirators' met in Francis Pym's room next to the Commons' changing rooms and barber's shop. Francis's reputation was high, particularly among the older Tory MPs. He had been Ted Heath's Chief Whip, responsible for the legislation which made the United Kingdom a member of the European Community. Under Margaret he had been Leader of the House and Defence and Foreign Secretary. Slight, dapper and intense, Pym lacked political magic. He also suffered grievously from indecision. Gilmour, who is perhaps the cleverest Tory of them all, was at his best wielding a pen. In the language of the prize-ring, he could box but he could not punch. Pym was nicknamed 'the Grand Old Duke of York', as time after time the public announcement of Centre Forward's existence was delayed. The conspirators met over a period of several months, on one occasion dining secretly in cellars beneath St James's Street.

Gilmour thought for the group, Peter Tapsell gave freely of his expertise in matters of economics, Charlie Morrison spoke for the knights of the shires. Alan Hazelhurst acted as whipper-in. I looked after the public relations and press relations.

I suggested that an invitation to attend be sent to Ted Heath. This was opposed successfully on the grounds that Ted was 'the kiss of death'. On his part, Heath was supposed to have been of the view that the exercise was probably doomed to failure. In the end we gave lunch in Basil Street for Peter Jenkins who at that time was the chief political correspondent of the *Sunday Times*, and Francis travelled to Oxford where he outlined to an audience in the Union, and to the cameras, the political philosophy of the anti-Thatcher Tories. The speech was immediately rubbished by Geoffrey Rippon who was the Maria Callas of the group. Pym, said Rippon, had put the emphasis in the wrong places, and had not listened closely to him. Mr Jeremy Hayes, a bearded newcomer, promptly announced his resignation from the group. Press publicity, which was universal, was inevitably over-shadowed by reports of defections. It was always a mystery why Rippon had been invited to join in the first place. An engaging man of considerable political distinction, he belonged to the traditional, pre-Thatcher right of the party. Hayes suffered from cold feet, a condition endemic among newcomers with ambition.

Pym had always been nervous at the prospect of Centre Forward being seen as a party within a party. That would, in the eyes of the Conservative establishment, have been a grievous sin. The group issued no whip of its own, and the then Chief Whip John Wakeham was to boast to Francis when the latter politely called upon him to tell him what was up, that he (the Government's Whips' Office) had known all along what was going on. He had certainly had a good idea. Wakeham had not penetrated the group but several of his juniors had got wind that something was afoot. There are few secrets at Westminster. In the event, Conservative Centre Forward was laughed into impotence, its members spending the rest of that parliament calling on ministers to make them aware of their concerns. Francis Pym did not seek re-election and the group died a political death.

Mrs Thatcher has always enjoyed the support, if not always the affection, of the bulk of the Conservative party. With her election as leader in '75, the Conservative party returned to its old allegiance, the 'tricolour' gave way to the lilies, and, with the defeat of Edward Heath, the line of the 'Churchill's' ceased to rule. Three separate intakes of Tory MPs have won their spurs under her leadership. Conservative MPs came increasingly to model themselves on the prevailing orthodoxy, for the wind, *pace* Chairman Mao, 'was from the East'. The East Midlands that is.

The party's MPs have lost a button off their cuff, an observation that was once made to me at table by an elderly knight of the shires, who hurried to explain that ready-made suits carried three, or even only two, buttons on their sleeves. It was not simply a case of 30 shillings well spent, the newcomers were Thatcherites almost to a man, a sombre mixture of garagistes, estate agents and graduates from the newer universities, whose political instincts were close to those of their leader. They are keen party conference goers. They want junior office in order to further the cause of the counter-revolution. They relish the passing on to the statute book of new legislation. In fact, the Tory party has, under Margaret, stopped being a party and become a movement, as dedicated to change as Labour itself once was. Manifestos have been written on tablets of stone. This sea change has put older Tories in some difficulty. We joined a party, not a movement, zeal was once left to our socialist opponents; today, it is hard to find a Tory who is not a zealot.

An attractive characteristic of the Prime Minister is her concern for the welfare of those who serve her. If she is tart it is only with her peers. She asks after the health of wives, and by name, and she can command the loyalty of those who work closely with her. A less attractive trait is her urge to dominate. She governs more like a President than a Prime Minister and if she leads, it is always from the front. She tends to dominate in small groups. She does not entertain; she instructs. She is didactic, preaching incessantly about the need to limit the power of government, and she extols the boundless power of the individual. Such conversational intensity does not make for fun, but Mrs Thatcher has never been a fun person. To find oneself sitting next to Harold Macmillan would be a delightful surprise. To be seated opposite Ted Heath would carry the risk of silence (much would depend upon his mood), but to be placed next to Margaret at dinner would demand the whole of one's attention. Crusaders, whatever their merits, are rarely comfortable travelling companions.

Mrs Thatcher is often compared with General de Gaulle. They are both major political figures, authoritarian, dogmatic, secretive and grand. De Gaulle was above all things an extreme nationalist, dedicated to la France, the self-interest of which he pursued to the point of mysticism. Mrs Thatcher is a British nationalist of a simpler sort who sees the European Common Market only in terms of the economic opportunities it might offer Britain, and as a candidate for the extension of Thatcherism. Her speech at Bruges in the summer of 1988 which was written by her private secretary, Charles Powell, seemed to set limits on the future political unity of Europe and by so doing to run the risk of Britain's isolation from the Continent.

The parallel with Charles de Gaulle (will a London underground station ever be named 'Margaret Thatcher'?) can be made to run but only so far. They are both nationalists. They are both authoritarian. They are both larger than life. But where de Gaulle was secretive, the same cannot be said of Mrs Thatcher. In the jargon of the media her profile is always high. The Prime Minister is admirably served by her press office, and in particular, by Mr Bernard Ingham. Sir Gordon Reece, the media man and 'magician' upon whose cosmetic advice Mrs Thatcher has long relied, is a Christmas Day guest of the Prime Minister's. Mrs Thatcher spends Christmas at Chequers. Lunch on Christmas Day is reserved for the most faithful members of her entourage: besides Reece there are Lord and Lady McAlpine, the party's treasurer, Sir Ronald Miller, whose task it is to provide a joke for the start of her annual party conference address, Mr Tim Bell, the advertising man, Sir Donald Gosling, the head of National Car Parks, the Mark Thatchers and Charles Powell and his wife. A traditional Christmas lunch is served, and there are no funny hats or crackers.

The Boxing Day lunch is a buffet. Once again, there are no funny hats or crackers. Last year's selection of guests included Peter Brooke, the Chairman of the Conservative party, the Jeffrey Archers, Sir Robin Butler, the cabinet secretary, and senior cabinet colleagues such as the Howes, the Majors, the Parkinsons and the Ridleys. There is always room for some of her

143

model businessmen such as Lord Hanson and John Bellak, the Chairman of the Severn and Trent Water Board. Although the event cannot be described as a gastronomic experience, invitations are much coveted. It would be fun to imagine that Mrs Thatcher draws the raffle. The two days of Christmas are given over to those who have earned the highest decoration Mrs Thatcher can bestow, and as her guest list shows, the Prime Minister has not been ungenerous with honours – that is, with membership of the Order of 'One of Us'. De Gaulle spent Christmas at Colombey les Deux Eglises alone, but with God.

What they do have in common are the unhappy circumstances which led to their taking power. De Gaulle most certainly arrested a drift in France towards anarchy and civil war. He told the crowd of *pieds noirs* in Algiers that he understood them; it soon became clear that he understood them only too well. The crisis in Algeria sent de Gaulle to the Elysée Palace. The winter of discontent in Britain made Mrs Thatcher's victory in May 1979. Earlier that year, James Callaghan, sniffing the air, said that he could sense a 'sea change' in British politics. Industrial unrest changed moods. That winter some few bodies lay unburied as a consequence of public sector strikes. There was a reaction against high inflation, high taxes, an expanding public sector and an atmosphere, encouraged by the press, of ungovernability. Labour had returned to the trade unions the privileges which Ted Heath had taken from them, and the trade union barons, the leaden-footed tigers of the Labour movement, were rarely silent, each of their utterances on television serving to boost the Conservative party's chances.

The picture ought not to be painted too garishly: there has been a tendency demonstrated by those with political axes to grind to re-write recent history, to claim that the pre-Thatcher years were a time of continual failure during which so-called Conservative Governments, led by out-of-touch grandees, flirted with corporatism in search of a quiet life, while Labour led inevitably to rack and ruin. Just as Mr Lawson's statistical base is 1981, thereby for purposes of debate disregarding the effects of the 1979/81 recession, so the supporters of the New Right have an interest in painting a darker picture than is merited by the events of the recent past. Had Callaghan gone to the country in the autumn of 1978, Labour would probably have won the general election.

Nevertheless, Mrs Thatcher was able to present herself to the country as a new broom, and her policies were novel enough to lend credibility to her boasting. There had been something tawdry about the Wilson years for which James Callaghan was to pay the price. De Gaulle buried the Fourth Republic; Mrs Thatcher has been the spokeswoman of Britain's populist counter-revolution. De Gaulle would have regarded Mrs Thatcher as a typical British politician who would, when asked to choose, always prefer the Anglo-American alliance to European unity, however defined. She might even have been described as 'the Trojan 'orse'. Where the comparison does break down is over de Gaulle's sense of history. Mrs Thatcher stands outside history. De Gaulle had a strong sense of history, a knowledge of the wider world and an intuitive feel for foreign affairs. De Gaulle was both Olympian and Delphic: Mrs Thatcher might be described as 'Olympian', but never as 'Delphic'. We know exactly where we stand.

Mrs Thatcher is perceived as a strong leader. It is easy to poke fun at her earnestness, and even easier to switch off the television before she has time to get into her stride. John Mortimer once asked 'why is she always so cross?', and she does tend to talk to the nation as if it deserved to be kept in after school. She is a great one for the pulling up of socks. But many people do like the smack of firm government and if we smart in consequence it will only serve to show how richly we have deserved chastisement. We remain, at heart, a Protestant people, wracked by guilt. Her message may not always be palatable, but it does have the virtue of being easy to understand. And it is all too simple to accept her list of 'enemies' as our own. Many people find her unlovable, but she does come across as being honest and straightforward.

I asked at the start of this chapter whether Mrs Thatcher deserved to be called 'Thatcherite'. In order to answer the question it is important that we know what precisely Thatcherism is supposed to be. Is it a term used simply to describe the set of moral attitudes which Mrs Thatcher has plainly made her own? And which she articulates in the language of home economics? Or is Thatcherism a synonym for 'neo-Conservatism'? Which is, in its turn, a synonym for the kind of Victorian liberalism once known as belonging to the Manchester School. Or is Thatcherism shorthand for the authoritarian and centralising beliefs which, while owing nothing whatever to neo-Conservatism, make up the most recognisable parts of the Thatcherite whole?

Neo-Conservatives whether American or British are believers in the virtues of competition. They worship the market, and do their level best to encourage market forces. They have no historical roots within the Tory party. In the nineteenth century Conservatives were hostile to commerce and the free market, and were the party of big public spending. 'Extravagance' was, according to Lord Blake, the biographer of Disraeli, 'a stock accusation made by Liberal economists against Conservative budgets.' As George Watson has written, few nineteenth-century Conservatives would have had a good word to say for the spirit of Reaganism/Thatcherism. They hated the prospect of a 'shopocracy' as something crude and vulgar. In *Coningsby* Disraeli openly derided the prospect of constituency-wide Conservative associations 'with a banker for its chairman, and a brewer for its vice-president'. Conservatives feared the results of competition which they saw as being profoundly un-conservative in effect. In 1988, Nicholas Ridley, a second son, who is on the neo-Conservative wing of the party, called for the taking over of great houses, once the property of 'old' money, by the new classes who have done well out of a decade of 'radical' Conservative government.

Competition is 'radical' in its social effects. Many of my richer constituents live in North Hampshire villages such as Hartley Wintney where they suffer from constant anxiety lest the physical effects of the policies which they ostensibly support at general elections serve to ruin their environment. More traffic jams, crowded commuter trains, gravel extraction, yobbery after dark, and an influx of outsiders buying up Charles Church's 'executive Georgian' houses are the sources of their not so private nightmares. One market they do not wish to be free is the market for new private houses.

Mrs Thatcher's rhetoric is often neo-Conservative, and many of her closest associates have been members of the New Right. (And, originally, of the New Left.) Yet she is also Statist in a sense which Disraeli himself might have recognised. There is a gulf between neo-Conservatism and Statism which any amount of speech-making cannot disguise. Monetary control is presented as an extension of the concept of the minimal state, and to the extent that it is based on lower public spending, it might be. But we have not had lower public spending. Fiscal control by unremitting centralised power is surely Statist in principle; and we are frequently assured by chancellors that control of the money supply is essential to the Conservative cause. High defence spending is Statist, and Mrs Thatcher, while welcoming the thaw in East/West relations, warns against Nato being lulled into a false sense of complacency. And for as long as American and British 'conservatives' insist upon Star Wars and Trident, it will be hard to reconcile their defence policies with monetary restraint.

The law to abolish the metropolitan boroughs, and notably the Greater London Council, forced through both Houses of Parliament in 1984, introduced a new and alarming principle into British politics, the right of central government to abolish elected bodies when it knows that it cannot win an election in the majority of them. The powers of local government have been severely curtailed in the name of economy. The theme of much of what Mrs Thatcher has achieved since 1979 has been 'power to the centre'. And this is as true of education as it is of local government.

Mrs Thatcher's political strength, although not necessarily her personal popularity which has, at times, dipped to levels unplumbed by any of her predecessors, is a factor of her apparent determination, her refusal 'to turn', or, at least to be seen to be doing so. She is a 'strong' leader. Given her victories over Galtieri, Scargill and her Conservative opponents, her reputation for possessing an unswerving sense of purpose remains a credible one. She wins a reluctant admiration for guts. Although Mrs Thatcher rejects what others would see as the accepted wisdom, for example she refuses to countenance the setting up of royal commissions which would be more than likely to reach conclusions that are unwelcome to her, 'Thatcherism' derives much of its strength from certain fundamentals of popular perceptions of what is right or wrong. Thatcherism is moralistic or it is nothing.

Let me list some of these perceptions:

Privileges must be earned, not inherited or assumed on the basis of some old boy network.

When a privilege has been earned, it is outrageous for anybody, including the tax collector, to take it away.

Books must be balanced and debt is sinful – the inheritance of Alderman Roberts.

The family is the unit of society ('there is no such thing as society'), and ideally all social welfare is a family responsibility.

While individuals should carry responsibility for failure, it is pointless for the community to feel guilt, and much bad legislation and bad government, in Mrs Thatcher's view, has resulted from trying to assuage collective guilt about unemployment, colonialism, homelessness, racial prejudice and poverty.

The ordinary citizen is entitled to feel righteous anger at the way he has been cheated over the years by the bumbling of the ruling classes, which by ignoring the commonsense propositions listed above have twisted the priorities of the nation. 'Thatcherism' is in essence anti-Establishment.

No sooner are these propositions listed than the paradoxes are evident. Neo-Conservatism, that is competition, has led to the excesses of the yuppie whose place in Britain is mirrored by that of the yob. It has also led to a credit-hungry society (so much for the sinfulness of debt) on an irresponsible scale, a phenomenon which has returned the government's economic policy to the 'stop/go' of the 'sixties and 'seventies. Nigel Lawson was Reggie Maudling but without Mr Poulson's swimming-pool.

By constant repetition, Mrs Thatcher has succeeded in turning the simplicities into verities. St Margaret is the patron saint of taxi drivers. She can also speak for the man in the street. In a famous interview shortly before she became Prime Minister, Mrs Thatcher told how her cabinet would have to be one 'that works on something more than consensus ... It must be a conviction Government. We've got to go in an agreed and clear direction. As Prime Minister I couldn't waste time having any internal arguments.' Yet, like Marxism, Thatcherism is, in fact, riddled with contradictions. Mrs Thatcher, on the other hand, is free of doubt, she is the label on the can of worms.

Perhaps the best way to sum up eleven years of Mrs Thatcher's rule is as follows: 'the Tory party has become Liberal but without being Gladstonian, populist without being popular.' Would we win a fourth general election under her leadership, given the return to two-party politics? There are surely only three likely outcomes: a '70, when Mr Heath snatched victory from defeat; a '64 when Labour was returned with a majority of three, and another '45. I hope for all our sakes we can do as well as Ted twenty years ago.

# *Index*